# FEATURE

AUTUMN 2024 • NUMBER

Plough

# DEPARTMENTS

# WEB EXCLUSIVES

Read these articles at *plough.com/web41*

## Plough

**ANOTHER LIFE IS POSSIBLE**

**EDITOR:** Peter Mommsen
**SENIOR EDITORS:** Shana Goodwin, Maria Hine,
Maureen Swinger, Sam Hine, Susannah Black Roberts
**EDITOR-AT-LARGE:** Caitrin Keiper
**BOOKS AND CULTURE EDITOR:** Joy Marie Clarkson
**POETRY EDITOR:** Jane Clark Scharl
**ASSOCIATE EDITORS:** Alan Koppschall, Madoc Cairns
**CONTRIBUTING EDITORS:** Leah Libresco Sargeant,
Brandon McGinley, Jake Meador, Santiago Ramos
**UK EDITION:** Ian Barth
**GERMAN EDITION:** Katharina Thonhauser
**COPY EDITORS:** Wilma Mommsen, Priscilla Jensen, Cameron Coombe
**DESIGNERS:** Rosalind Stevenson, Miriam Burleson
**MARKETING DIRECTOR:** Tim O'Connell
**FOUNDING EDITOR:** Eberhard Arnold (1883–1935)
Plough Quarterly No. 41: Freedom
Published by Plough Publishing House, ISBN 978-1-63608-160-1
Copyright © 2024 by Plough Publishing House. All rights reserved.

**EDITORIAL OFFICE**
151 Bowne Drive
Walden, NY 12586
T: 845.572.3455
info@plough.com

**SUBSCRIBER SERVICES**
PO Box 8542
Big Sandy, TX 75755
T: 800.521.8011
subscriptions@plough.com

United Kingdom
Brightling Road
Robertsbridge
TN32 5DR
T: +44(0)1580.883.344

Australia
4188 Gwydir Highway
Elsmore, NSW
2360 Australia
T: +61(0)2.6723.2213

Plough Quarterly (ISSN 2372-2584) is published quarterly by
Plough Publishing House, PO Box 398, Walden, NY 12586.
Individual subscription $36 / £24 / €28 per year.
Subscribers outside of the United States and Canada pay in British pounds or euros.
Periodicals postage paid at Walden, NY 12586 and at additional mailing offices.
POSTMASTER: Send address changes to Plough Quarterly, PO Box 8542, Big Sandy, TX 75755.

Front cover: *Exodo*, oil on canvas, 2022, Julio Larraz© Reproduced with permission
of Julio Larraz and Havoli Fine Art Management, Inc.
Inside front cover: Zinaida Serabriakova, *Green Autumn*, oil on canvas, 1908. Used by permission.
Back cover: Andrew Wyeth, *Deserted Light*, watercolor and pencil, 1977. © 2024 Wyeth Foundation
for American Art / Artists Rights Society (ARS), New York. Used by permisison.

### ABOUT THE COVER
The characters in Cuban artist Julio Larraz's
*Exodo* experience both the beauty and
the danger of freedom – their little boat
is set adrift in a world without guides or
boundaries, and they are compelled to take
up the oars and chart a clear course.

# LETTERS

Readers respond to *Plough's* Summer 2024 issue, *The Good of Tech*. Send letters to *letters@ plough.com.*

## SHOULD WE LISTEN TO AI SERMONS?

*On Arlie Coles's "ChatGPT Goes to Church":* You posit the question incorrectly. It's not "Should ChatGPT write sermons?" Rather "Can we tell when it does?"

Harried clergy run out of time during the week. They get burned out. Or sick. Or spiritually depleted. Supply clergy may be unavailable at the last minute. Fresh, new approaches to interpreting scripture can elude the most earnest soul at times. Reworking that incisive commentary on Romans, delivered two years prior, is not a palatable alternative. The temptation to fulfill the exhortation "the show must go on" will, for at least some shepherds, overwhelm their moral scruples.

Congregants, awaken to the new reality. AI-generated sermons will eventually descend to a pulpit near you. Ironically, sermons form a wonderfully rich training base for building a large language model (LLM) database, perhaps the best imaginable, given the volume, scholarship, and quality of the writing. There are millions of sermons floating around the internet, freely available and easy to upload. The Bible, Talmud, Quran, Bhagavad Gita and most every other book of faith is an easy upload as well.

Within a year or two, LLM-based machines will become so mellifluous, so compelling, so penetrating in reaching our hearts and minds that humans won't be able to tell the difference between machine-generated content and the organic variety. Virtually every creative industry – art, entertainment, education – is being overrun with AI-generated content right now. Why would faith be inviolate?

*Charles Sullivan, Gaithersburg, Maryland*

It should be simply intuitive as a minister of God to know that using AI to write a sermon isn't OK. God speaks into each new day and he speaks to his servants who are listening for him. In order for a word from the Lord to be fresh and relevant a human, not a machine created by humans, needs to be hearing directly from the Holy Spirit. Otherwise, what you are feeding your flock is processed food. Junk food. Unhealthy shelf-stable dead food.

Discerning sheep will refuse to eat this junk food. They will search for new pasture if it isn't provided. God's not dead. AI is only as good as its programming and it is never moved by the Holy Spirit. Only man can accomplish this. And it's a sacred privilege to be called to serve God's people. God does not consult with his creation before instructing it. Yet man thinks his inventions should be consulted to instruct man? Does anyone see a problem here besides me?

*Xenia Esche, Newman Lake, Washington*

## THE CHALLENGE TO DISCERN

*On Peter Berkman's "Machine Apocalypse":* This article took me a while to digest and left me feeling challenged to keep attempting to unveil the realities under the surface of everyday life. As a youth worker it felt overwhelming to realize that the young people I work with have been born into a different context/reality/metaphysics than me – and also that the need for them to be able to discern the mechanics of this reality, and find ways of developing an ethic to keep up with its power, will only increase with time.

*Miranda Haslem, London, England*

## NIP AND TUCK

*On Brian Miller's "Give Me a Place":* Having worked as a college boy on the railroad back in the 1970s (not *for* the railroad but *on* the railroad, I like to say – and in Louisiana), I was taught to call it a "lining bar" or a "nipping bar." The sharper end was thrust into a wooden crosstie and the bar was used to "nip" the tie up enough to then shovel dirt and gravel underneath it. Such nipping and tucking could eventuate in such a solid, immovable situation with the crosstie that the track seemed mounted on a concrete foundation. But "rock bar" or "tamping bar" sure does describe what most of us use them for now. Thank you and thank God for rock bars.

*Chip Prehn, Sisterdale, Texas*

## GOD'S TIMING

*On Lydia S. Dugdale's "It's Getting Harder to Die":* My wife Anne died in the year 2000 of motor neuron disease at the age of thirty-five. As Christians, we did not believe in euthanasia, as this is to take God's place. We wanted it to happen in the Lord's timing, not man's, so we were committed to palliative care only. However, this was not easily acceptable by the medical profession, and we had to fight them all the way. As Christians, we need to advocate for people to be allowed to die, without unnecessary life extension. As a footnote: Anne died peacefully at home with me and our son.

*Nigel Parrott, Kiviõli, Estonia*

## THE IMPORTANCE OF LISTENING

*On Brewer Eberly's "In Defense of Human Doctors":* As a child, I got to know our family doctor as a friend, one who listened to this little girl with her silly complaints. From him I learned the importance of listening. When I had my own children, he did their routine check-ups. The thought of this

caring, face-to-face exchange being cut out of an appointment makes me cross. We are human beings; we need a caring person talking to us. If AI robot doctors take over, there will be an increase in loneliness and worse, I am sure.

*Ruth Ann Gattis, Robertsbridge, England*

## THE COLD TRUTH

*On Haley Stewart's "The Case for Not Sanitizing Fairy Tales":* No matter how often you reassert the premise that kids need the unadulterated versions of fairy tales, I'm stuck on the images of Cinderella's stepsisters and their bloody feet, the Little Mermaid facing either death or becoming a murderer. Are we really talking about those images as salutary no matter what comes next? I'm imagining Jesus portraying the Prodigal Son stumbling home eyes sunken, hair coming out in patches, teeth falling out from malnutrition. Because, you know, that's the cold truth. I affirm communicating to kids at age-appropriate levels – in part dictated by their developing capacities to take the lessons on board – of truth, mystery, meaning out of the seeming chaos of the world surrounding us. I do not believe the author makes her case that the original stories gathered and published in 1812 ought to be treated as some sort of quasi-sacred texts.

Kids in 2024 have enough to be anxious about.

*Grant Barber, Whitman, Massachusetts*

## IS DE-MACHINING WORTH IT?

*On Tara Isabella Burton's "Simple Steps to Combat Smartphone Addiction":* This comes dangerously close to sounding like an Apple Watch ad. I appreciate what you've said though, about your breakthrough happening when you *added* enriching commitments to your life rather than merely *taking away* the smartphone.

*Kelly Endicott, Half Moon Bay, California*

Like so many people, I too struggle with trying to limit the phone and not being present in the real world. For the past year and a half I have been trying to de-machine my life as much as possible while being realistic in my aims. I gave up online shopping for Lent this year and that was a revelation. Why am I ordering scotch tape on Amazon? The takeaway is that you have to do these new (actually old) ways for at least a month for them to change your habits and it is well worth it. Onward and upward!

*Amy Nolan, St. Joseph, Michigan*

## The Forgiveness Project

*In London, an unconventional project shares stories of forgiveness.*

### Marina Cantacuzino

This year marks twenty years since I founded The Forgiveness Project. It seems ironic that a charity whose foundation lies in compassion, empathy, and forgiveness was actually driven by anger. In February 2003 I was on a peace march in London protesting loudly against the imminent invasion of Iraq, convinced that the harder you come down on people the more they will regroup in a more vengeful and resistant way. I was appalled by the divisive language of polarization, by the assumption that "if you're not with us you're against us." For this reason, as a journalist, I started to collect stories that were countercultural, a deliberate antidote to the pervasive narratives of demonization and hate.

These stories, from victims and perpetrators, became *The F Word* – an exhibition of individuals who had reconciled with pain by drawing a line under the dogma of vengeance. They demonstrated how people

had sought peaceful solutions to conflict and found meaning in their suffering. As stated by one of the storytellers (a former gang member from Los Angeles whose son was killed in youth violence), "Where the wounds are, the gift lies."

I called these testimonies restorative narratives; they seemed to tap into a deep public need to find hope in places of despair. The astonishing success of the exhibition led me to founding The Forgiveness Project – a charity that collects and shares personal stories. Our purpose is to demonstrate how individuals and groups can break cycles of pain, reach across division, and find humanity in others.

During the past twenty years we've been working with storytellers from around the globe through our prison program, school resource, exhibitions, seminars, and courses. We've profiled our work in the media, academic research, arts projects, podcasts, and books. We continue to do this work because of the countless people who have said that The Forgiveness Project has helped them make sense of their own lives, encouraged them to reconcile after estrangement, or shed light on the heartache in the world.

We don't attempt to persuade people that they must forgive in order to free themselves from the tangle of hate. Rather, we present alternatives to the cycle of revenge. In fact, forgiveness may be costly, untimely, or inappropriate in certain circumstances. As Julie Nicholson, whose daughter was killed in the London bombings on July 7, 2005, has said: "The

whole area of forgiveness is like a huge spectrum. . . . At one end you have a fracas in the playground, and at the other end you've got mass slaughter, and yet you've got this one word that is supposed to fit everything."

My favorite description of forgiveness is attributed to the American author Mark Twain: "Forgiveness is the fragrance that the violet sheds on the heel that has crushed it." Forgiveness is messy. It grows out of damage, but is also a healing balm. I've learned that the pull to forgive is flexible and changeable, not a one-size-fits-all, nor a single magnanimous gesture in response to an isolated offense. Rather, it is fluid and forever changing, just like the definitions endeavoring to describe it.

Today, with the Israel-Palestine conflict creating a cauldron of blame and competing narratives, such is the level of mistrust and fury that it is hard to imagine forgiveness ever being used as a tool for repair. However, once again, I feel an urgent need to tap into the power of storytelling, because I know firsthand how stories that focus on compassion and connection can change mindsets and enable us to embrace new perspectives.

From the restorative narratives that The Forgiveness Project has collected and shared over many years, there is one critical ingredient to forgiveness that might be of use in this present climate – curiosity. Of course, being curious about your enemy is difficult when people feel threatened, but at an event in London last December, Robi Damelin, a bereaved mother from the

---

*Marina Cantacuzino is the founder of The Forgiveness Project.* theforgivenessproject.com.

Israel-Palestine group the Parents Circle Families Forum, encouraged the audience to stop holding with such certainty to their opinions, and instead reach out and explore the story of perhaps a single Palestinian under siege in Gaza or one Israeli hostage. In a world where bystanders have taken sides, she urged us to rehumanize the other by staying curious about different perspectives. This means that while we still feel the anger and hurt, we learn to respond out of compassion rather than rage.

This curiosity, this empathy, is a quality that embraces a forgiving mindset, accepting that people aren't simply bad or wrong just because their opinions are diametrically opposed to your own. It requires imagining what it is like to be someone other than yourself, which is never easy. As Plato concluded almost two and a half millennia ago, "The highest form of knowledge is empathy, for it requires us to suspend our egos and live in another's world." ➔

## Humanizing Medicine

*In Baltimore, the Paul McHugh Program for Human Flourishing gets med students talking.*

### Margaret S. Chisolm

Studying medicine forces students in health professions to grapple directly with philosophical questions. These include questions about the nature of being human, the essence of health and healing, the role of suffering, and what it means to live well and die well. They are questions that the world's religious traditions have offered responses to for thousands of years. Yet the young adults who are studying for different health professions belong primarily to Gen Z, thirty-four percent of whom have no religious affiliation. Given the growing lack of religious connection and the near absence of exposure to religion in American public education, these young students need guidance as they confront the big questions.

How do we help students consider what the world's faith traditions teach about these questions? How do we help them understand that virtues might make them better people (and health professionals)? At the Paul McHugh Program for Human Flourishing we try to help students at Johns Hopkins University (and beyond) to do just that. We guide them through many different types of arts and humanities activities, all designed to stimulate reflection on the big questions and help them flourish as health professionals. Our ultimate goal is for students to experience the awe-some nature of medicine. It is an incredible privilege to encounter another human being in the midst of suffering and to offer that person hope and healing.

Since 2015, the McHugh Program has developed and launched a number of arts and humanities initiatives for students in health professions. One of these, the Longitudinal Scholars Program (LSP) in Human Flourishing, provides individual and group mentorship to a select group of students through all four years of medical school, and beyond. In addition to the LSP, the McHugh Program offers courses open to any Hopkins pre-health or medical student. These courses are all grounded in Tyler VanderWeele's model of human flourishing and taught entirely in art museums, where students use art to explore how family, religious community, education, and work are pathways to a flourishing life. For example, one activity requires students to walk individually through the galleries and select an artwork that represents their motivation to become a health professional. The students spend a few minutes sketching the artwork and reflecting in writing on their choice. Then the students come together to tour

*Margaret S. Chisolm, MD, is a professor of psychiatry at Johns Hopkins University and the director of the Paul McHugh Program for Human Flourishing.*

The author leads a Visual Thinking Strategies discussion at the National Gallery of Art.

## About Us

*Plough* is published by the Bruderhof, an international community of families and singles seeking to follow Jesus together. Members of the Bruderhof are committed to a way of radical discipleship in the spirit of the Sermon on the Mount. Inspired by the first church in Jerusalem (Acts 2 and 4), they renounce private property and share everything in common in a life of nonviolence, justice, and service to neighbors near and far. There are twenty-nine Bruderhof settlements in both rural and urban locations in the United States, England, Germany, Australia, Paraguay, South Korea, and Austria, with around 3000 people in all. To learn more or arrange a visit, see the community's website at *bruderhof.com*.

*Plough* features original stories, ideas, and culture to inspire faith and action. Starting from the conviction that the teachings and example of Jesus can transform and renew our world, we aim to apply them to all aspects of life, seeking common ground with all people of goodwill regardless of creed. The goal of *Plough* is to build a living network of readers, contributors, and practitioners so that, as we read in Hebrews, we may "spur one another on toward love and good deeds."

*Plough* includes contributions that we believe are worthy of our readers' consideration, whether or not we fully agree with them. Views expressed by contributors are their own and do not necessarily reflect the editorial position of *Plough* or of the Bruderhof communities. ➤

the galleries, sharing the artwork they picked with each other and commenting on its connection to their professional identity. Such activities increase our students' capacity for wonder, tolerance of ambiguity, and ability to empathize with patients. They grow both personally and professionally. Here the students speak for themselves:

"Overall, I am surprised at the very positive impact this course has had on me and my perspectives. I connected with the art and fellow members of the course at a deeper level than I had anticipated, and I look forward to continuing to look for such connections in the future. I am pleased to say this course has been a real highlight of my medical education thus far and I expect the lessons learned will help me become a more empathic and effective physician and overall person."

"The course reinforced my values. It never felt like there were values placed upon us, but so many activities asked us to evaluate who we were, how we felt, and what we wanted that it became a space to critically think about our values and whether we were living by them."

"I've been surprised by how much I've been stretched by this course. I've been forced to interrogate prejudices and limits to empathy that I didn't realize I had. I've learned that art has a unique ability to inspire vulnerable reflections that show me more about who I am and take me by surprise."

"I gained an incredible energy, peace, and joy from taking this course, so much so that I wept after our last session. I am so grateful to have taken this course when I did and I'm dejected now that it's over. I feel more hope for my future as a physician, and more confidence in my abilities to face the future."

The McHugh Program is now seeking funding to support the launch of additional museum-based courses for both pre-health and medical students. We have a particular interest in courses focused on religion and spirituality and the related concepts of awe and wonder. Students will encounter, reflect on, and discuss paintings, household objects, music, stories, poems, and ritual and devotional objects that have emerged from Christianity, Judaism, Islam, Buddhism, and Hinduism. In addition, they will participate in art-making activities – sketching, mask-making, reflective writing – related to religious traditions and healing within those traditions. Students will explore questions: Is there a divine reality? How is it related to the cosmos, and how can we know it better? How can we become better thinkers and inquirers? How do we improve our ways of learning about and understanding the world? What can we learn from the world's religious traditions about fundamental spiritual realities? Students will also reflect on their personal relationship (or that of their family or community) with any religious and spiritual tradition – if they have one. Through these courses, we hope to understand better the growing number of "spiritual-but-not religious" young adults and how their spiritual searches might relate to flourishing. ➤

# In Defiance of All Powers

*What's the point of freedom?*

**PETER MOMMSEN**

"FREEDOM!" was what Hans Scholl and two fellow students painted on walls around Munich during the night of February 3, 1943. The three friends, all in their twenties, were members of the anti-Nazi movement known as the *Weiße Rose* or White Rose. They painted the word freehand, three feet high, using tar-based black paint that would be tough to scrub away. For their other slogans – "Down with Hitler" and "Hitler the Mass Murderer" – they used stencils.

Two of them did the work while the third stood guard with a pistol.

Since the summer before, Hans Scholl and other members of the White Rose had been writing and distributing illegal leaflets that demanded, "Freedom! Freedom! Freedom!" These short manifestos condemned "National Socialist subhumanism," decried the war and the German extermination campaign against Poland's Jews, and called for resistance and sabotage. By this

Julio Larraz, *The Big Fish*, oil on canvas, 2009.

point, the group had access to a duplicating machine and was anonymously distributing thousands of copies in public places and by mail, as well as through their networks in other cities. Hans Scholl served in the army as a medic during academic breaks, and had seen firsthand the horrors of the Eastern Front. The midnight graffiti campaign was the White Rose's response to Germany's loss of its Sixth Army at Stalingrad, where at least 1.2 million people, including 200,000 German soldiers, had died.

On a morning two weeks later, Hans and his twenty-one-year-old sister, Sophie, set out to distribute the White Rose's sixth and last leaflet on the University of Munich campus. "Fellow Students!" it began. "Devastated, our nation stands before the downfall of the men of Stalingrad. . . . The day of reckoning has come, the reckoning of our German youth with the most despicable tyranny ever endured by our nation. In the name of all German youth, we demand from Adolf Hitler's state our personal freedom. . . . Our nation is on the verge of rising up against the enslavement of Europe through National Socialism, in the new, devoutly believing breakthrough of freedom and honor!"

When they had placed most of their 1,500 leaflets in stacks around campus, Sophie, on impulse, tossed a pile of copies down from the balustrade in the atrium of a university hall. A janitor saw her,

locked the building, and called the police. She and Hans were arrested by the Gestapo on the spot. He remembered too late that his pocket contained the draft of a seventh leaflet by his friend Christoph Probst. The Gestapo seized Probst, also a student and a father of three, shortly afterward. Four days after the initial arrest, the three were condemned to death for treason in a two-hour trial and executed. (Other White Rose members, including Hans's fellow graffitists Willi Graf and Alexander Schmorell, would be executed over the following months.) In court, Hans Scholl insisted that he had acted freely: "I knew what I took upon myself and I was prepared to lose my life by so doing."

I N THIS YEAR'S presidential election contest in the United States, both candidates have made much of the word *freedom*. "We choose freedom," Kamala Harris announced in her first campaign video, vowing to protect access to abortion, combat gun violence, fight poverty, and ensure that "no one is above the rule of law"; Beyoncé's "Freedom," a favorite song at Harris rallies, is the video's soundtrack. Donald Trump, meanwhile, promises in his platform to defend "our fundamental freedoms, including freedom of speech, freedom of religion, and the right to keep and bear arms." He has spoken of building ten new "freedom cities" that are exempt from government regulations.

Hans Scholl, Sophie Scholl, and Christoph Probst.

Clearly, "freedom" can mean many things, not all of them compatible with each other. Both candidates' appeals to freedom, all the same, do share a common core in asserting the American ideal of self-determination. But self-determination for what? Which kinds of freedom might be worth dying for?

WE MODERNS TEND to understand freedom as being defined in the negative: not being dominated. Freedom means chains being broken, slaves being emancipated, oppressors and busybodies losing their power. It is liberation from tyrannical governments, self-aggrandizing elites, and the enforcers of strict social codes.

This kind of freedom lies at the heart of liberal democracy, rooted in the Enlightenment. It is the grand theme of the French Revolution's Declaration of the Rights of Man and of the Citizen, drafted in 1789 by the Marquis de Lafayette with help from Thomas Jefferson: "Men are born free and equal in rights. . . . Liberty consists in being able to do anything that does not harm others."

These ringing words, which would prove massively influential in the development of "free" societies, have an undoubted majesty. As a political ideal, they accord with, and arguably derive from, Christianity's teaching that each human being is created in the image of God, whose very essence (according to the New Testament) is freedom. To be a human being, then, simply *is* to be born free. As Jefferson had put it thirteen years earlier in the American Declaration of Independence, it means possessing an "unalienable right" to liberty as a gift of humankind's Creator.

It was in the name of this revolutionary freedom that the White Rose resisted the "enslavement of Europe." Their leaflets called for the civil liberties that are foundational to liberal democracy, including freedom of speech and religion, academic freedom, and "freedom of the individual citizen from despotism."

But this kind of freedom is incomplete. Though Hans and Sophie Scholl risked their lives for it, they recognized that political freedom, on its own, remains impoverished. Influenced by Catholic mentors such as Carl Muth and Theodor Haecker, they had immersed themselves in the writings of Augustine and Aquinas. From them, they had learned a vision of freedom that was deeper, richer, and more ancient.

Freedom, according to these thinkers, is not only freedom *from* external domination or constraint. Equally important is freedom *to:* our internal capacity to act. This requires self-rule, self-mastery, the overcoming of the divided will, of *akrasia*, as Greek philosophers and the Bible call it. This freedom can't be granted to a person by a government or anyone else, but must be cultivated in one's own life.

Since for many people today this kind of freedom is no longer intuitive, it can be useful to consider an example. Take a skillful violinist playing a Bach partita. His freedom to play is found in the very act of playing. This freedom doesn't come from external circumstances – say, not being handcuffed, having the political right to make music, or owning an instrument. Instead, as my teenage son is now tired of hearing because he just wants to go fishing, freedom to play the violin comes from commitment. It is won through submitting oneself to what may initially seem like freedom's opposite: lessons, practice, discipline. The renowned conductor Serge Koussevitzky, though he was remembered by his protégé Leonard Bernstein as "a very kind, gentle man," used to tell players, "You must *suffer*. Why don't you suffer more? Only then will the music be beautiful."

In his letters, Hans Scholl describes "moral" or "spiritual" freedom, a freedom that doesn't depend on external circumstances, including the political regime in which one lives. As he wrote in his diary in August 1942 while on the Russian front: "I know how limited human freedom is, but man is essentially free, and it is his freedom that renders him human." This essential freedom is a way of being that one can make one's own "in defiance of all powers" – words from a Goethe poem about freedom that the Scholl family used as a motto. Or as Hans put it in what can be taken as his guiding principle: "Live life to the full, or not at all."

HOW CAN A PERSON GAIN this freedom? In his 1996 novel *Infinite Jest,* David Foster Wallace describes one way. The book chronicles the lives of characters variously addicted to sports, chemicals, entertainment, and sex. One of these is Don Gately, a resident at an Alcoholics Anonymous rehab house in Boston. He struggles with the *akrasia* of a substance abuser: "Why can't I quit when I so want to quit?"

> It's suggested in the 3rd of Boston AA's 12 Steps that you turn your Diseased will over to the direction and love of 'God as you understand Him.' It's supposed to be one of AA's major selling points that you get to choose your own God. You get to make up your own understanding of God or a Higher Power or Whom-/Whatever. . . . You might think it'd be easier if you Came In with 0 in the way of denominational background or preconceptions, you might think it'd be easier to sort of invent a Higher-Powerish God from scratch and then like erect an understanding, but Don Gately complains that this has not been his experience thus far. His sole experience so far is that he takes one of AA's very rare specific suggestions and hits the knees in the A.M. and asks for Help and then hits the knees again at bedtime and says Thank You, whether he believes he's talking to Anything/-body or not, and he somehow gets through that day clean.

For Gately, AA's prescriptions work, as he finds after several months in the program:

> He had nothing in the way of a like God-concept, and at that point maybe even less than nothing in terms of interest in the whole thing; he treated

prayer like setting an oven-temp according to a box's direction. Thinking of it as talking to the ceiling was somehow preferable to imagining talking to Nothing. And he found it embarrassing to get down on his knees in his underwear, and like the other guys in the room he always pretended his sneakers were like way under the bed and he had to stay down there a while to find them and get them out, when he prayed, but he did it, and beseeched the ceiling and thanked the ceiling, and after maybe five months Gately . . . all of a sudden realized that quite a few days had gone by since he'd even thought about Demerol or Talwin or even weed. Not just merely getting through those last few days – Substances hadn't even occurred to him. I.e. the Desire and Compulsion had been Removed. More weeks went by, a blur of Commitments and meetings and gasper-smoke and clichés, and he still didn't feel anything like his old need to get high. He was, in a way, Free. It was the first time he'd been out of this kind of mental cage since he was maybe ten. He couldn't believe it.

For Gately – as for countless nonfictional participants in twelve-step programs ever since AA's founding in 1935 – freedom arrives paradoxically: through submitting to Another.

David Foster Wallace's views on religion were complicated. But as many of his readers have noted, his portrayal of Gately's recovery echoes a central New Testament text on freedom. (This is hardly coincidental, because real-life Alcoholics Anonymous, though not religiously affiliated, originally emerged from the Oxford Group, a Christian revivalist movement.) In his Letter to the Romans, the apostle Paul struggles with the same dilemma that drove Gately to rehab: Why can't I quit when I so want to quit?

> I have the desire to do what is right, but not the ability to carry it out. For I do not do the good I want, but the evil I do not want is what I keep on doing. . . . For I delight in the law of God, in my inner being, but I see in my members another

law waging war against the law of my mind and making me captive to the law of sin that dwells in my members. Wretched man that I am! Who will deliver me from this body of death? (Rom. 7:18–19, 22–24)

To put it anachronistically, for Paul the "law of sin" is a kind of addiction. It deprives us of our unalienable birthright of freedom, robbing us of our capacity to do what we truly want. Liberation from this "slavery" requires the first two of the twelve steps: honesty about one's own powerlessness, and turning to a Higher Power for help. As he describes the means of recovery: "Thanks be to God, that you who were once slaves of sin have become obedient from the heart to the standard of teaching to which you were committed, and, having been set free from sin, have become slaves of righteousness" (Rom. 6:17–18).

In Paul's view, we will be free not when we choose whatever we might happen to desire, but when we will as God wills – that is, when we love, in the sense of Jesus' two great commandments to love God with heart, soul, mind, and strength, and to love our neighbor as ourselves. Augustine later condensed these insights into his famous aphorism: "Love and do what you will." As felt in the soaring notes of a violin, this kind of commitment expands, rather than limits, our souls.

It's remarkable how explicitly the members of the White Rose, even while defending political liberty, emphasized freedom's spiritual roots in ways that echo the New Testament. Their fourth leaflet diagnoses the evil of National Socialism as a kind of addiction – one bad choice leading to a loss of the ability to quit – and seems to suggest that the cure requires the intervention of a Higher Power:

Julio Larraz, *Falcon Aboard*, oil on canvas, 2000.

Everywhere and at all times demons have been lurking in the dark, waiting for the moment when man is weak; when of his own volition he leaves his place in the order of creation as founded for him by God in freedom; when he yields to the force of evil, separates himself from the powers of a higher order; and, after voluntarily taking the first step, he is driven on to the next and the next at a furiously accelerating rate. Everywhere and at all times of greatest trial people have appeared, prophets and saints who cherished their freedom, who preached the one God and who with his help brought the people to a reversal of their downward course. Man is free, to be sure, but without the true God he is defenseless against the principle of evil.

Even in political affairs, the leaflet argues, freedom is not achieved purely by our own efforts. It comes as a gift from a Giver, who calls for our free obedience in return. As Augustine and Aquinas had taught, the closer we come to the Giver of freedom – the more we love what he loves and will what he wills – the freer we become.

THIS KIND OF FREEDOM doesn't depend on a political order or even one's physical liberty. It's possible even in a prison cell.

After their brief trial on the morning of February 22, 1943, Hans Scholl, Sophie Scholl, and Christoph Probst heard their death sentence at 12:45 p.m. The authorities in Berlin were eager for the sentence to be carried out that same day. The local *Gauleiter* commissioned a carpenter to build gallows for a public hanging, but was overridden by Heinrich Himmler, who worried about making the students into martyrs.

In prison, where they spent their last three hours, Christoph received baptism and communion from a Catholic priest. Hans and Sophie wanted to do the same, but held back out of respect for their devoutly Lutheran mother, and instead received communion from the Protestant prison pastor.

At four o'clock, the three were informed that a final appeal for clemency had been denied, and that the execution would be at five.

Shortly beforehand, the prison guards waived their own rules and allowed the three to share a last cigarette. The Scholl siblings had been able to say farewell to their parents. Christoph, whose wife was unaware of her husband's fate (she was in hospital with childbed fever), now knew that he would never see his four-week-old daughter. All the same, he seems to have been at peace. When it was time to say goodbye, the guards would later recall him saying to the others, "In a few minutes we'll see each other again in eternity."

Sophie was taken to the guillotine first; Christoph was to be last. Two minutes after she had gone, the guards came for Hans. The official record of execution notes that the time elapsed between removal from the cell and death was fifty-two seconds and that "the condemned was tranquil and composed." It adds: "His last words were, 'Long live freedom!'"

The previous October, Sophie, in a letter to a friend, sketched out her own sense of what freedom is for. We are, she suggested, to use the freedom the Creator has given us to choose the beauty of his plan for ourselves and for the world. Despite the horrors of human history, she was confident this plan would prevail:

Isn't it mysterious – and frightening, too, when one doesn't know the reason – that everything should be so beautiful in spite of the terrible things that are happening? My sheer delight in all things beautiful has been invaded by a great unknown, an inkling of the Creator whom his creatures glorify with their beauty. – That's why man alone can be ugly, because he has the free will to disassociate himself from this song of praise. Nowadays one is often tempted to believe that he'll drown the song with gunfire and curses and blasphemy. But it dawned on me last spring that he can't, and I'll try to take the winning side. ➤

**JORDAN CASTRO**

# Heroin and Fiction

*I sought freedom in drugs and novels. But they couldn't save me.*

SIMONE DE BEAUVOIR WROTE that novels are compelling to the degree that the characters in them actually seem free. Novels in which the reader has a sense that the characters have agency, make decisions, and aren't mere instantiations of ideologies or "types" are better than novels in which characters follow predictably plotted paths. Of course, characters in a novel aren't free – they're printed words, contained between two covers – but, for Beauvoir, this illusion of freedom is what gives novels life. Raskolnikov is going to confess no matter who is reading *Crime and Punishment*, but for the specific, individual, first-time reader, Raskolnikov might, *or he might not*. The illusion of freedom, and the reader's participation in this illusion, is what compels the reader, and allows him to participate in the process more fully.

In novels, as in youth, the sense that you can do anything feels exciting. A lack of certain knowledge of the future, the open possibility of myriad options, contributes to the sense that one is free. The future is not a wall, or even a path, but a door, many doors, scattered about, which lead to unknown places, through which a man can enter or exit as he pleases – or stay completely still, whatever suits him. This sense that *anything can happen* is exciting.

But of course, not everything, and not just anything, can happen. If we want the novel to read well, or our life to go well, our options start to slim. We are free in some ways, but in others we are painfully constrained. I can't flap my arms and fly, for example. The same applies to moral and spiritual reality. There are things that *thou shalt not*, and things that *thou shalt*. The path is narrow. We are characters in the great drama written by the author of life; free to stray from the logic of the story – from what is proper given our personhood, circumstance, and so on – but when we do, this makes for something incoherent and unreadable. The great mystery of choice – which in novels is illusory, but in life I think is real – has consequences for our sense of freedom or lack thereof.

Novels temporarily free us from decision-making, or what the philosopher Yi-Ping Ong calls "deliberative reflection." In life, there are few, if any, thoughts that are not also tied up in choice, in our sense of identity, and in existential concerns that semiconsciously affect how we think. A human is conscious, but his consciousness is bound up in his life – in himself – and so he is not free to reflect in an objective way on consciousness itself, or at least not his own. A person thinks he observes himself, or knows himself, but often an outside observer can see things about him that are glaringly obvious, but that he remains blind to. When thinking, we are

motivated by many deliberative concerns, yet this component of our thought gets largely sidelined when reading fiction. While we read, we exist in a kind of limbo; another consciousness enters into ours and temporarily replaces it.

In order to read, the reader must die. Realist novels in particular, Yi-Ping Ong writes, create "a situation in which lived experience is made known from the point of view of a participant without the . . . reader . . . thereby being burdened by the responsibility that she would normally take up by claiming this knowledge." The reader adopts a new consciousness, one which does not involve her own self-interested will. She is born again as the fictional narrator or protagonist in front of her, a "consciousness" in a pre-plotted life – which feels alive – created by a distant author. Here, free will is an illusion. We submit ourselves to something other than ourselves, yet this submission can also be an eschewal of responsibility – responsibility to weigh options, to discern, to *choose* – and this can turn into compulsive escapism or worse. "Literature," Fernando Pessoa wrote, "is the most agreeable way of ignoring life."

This was, I think, partly what drew me to novels at a young age. I was attracted to books that spoke to my adolescent confusion and pain, ones I could safely identify with. The novels I loved portrayed a particular texture of consciousness that I could adopt momentarily and "try on" but that also enabled me to drift into morbid reflection, resting noncommittally in the hazy space between thought and action. Reading and thinking *felt like action*. I'd sit on my bed or the floor, my eyes the only part of me moving, left to right across the page. I'd skip school to read; I didn't care about others' interpretations of works. I acted as if I was frozen in a block of ice in a dark room, stuck with no path out; no windows above or around to look out of, just the page; no warmth to melt what froze me there, no life.

Moreover, despite literature's unique capacity to

*Jordan Castro is a writer and editor who lives in New York City. His most recent book is* The Novelist.

give me insight into *the other*, I couldn't actually escape myself. I projected myself onto characters, situations, dilemmas. Michael W. Clune notes that his literature students often write about things in the text that aren't really there. They bring themselves to the text in such a way that they're not really reading the words on the page but rather projecting meanings onto it. A single word might become a tiny reflection of oneself, a paragraph a hall of funhouse mirrors.

So my reading was some soupy mix of escape into another consciousness and projection, in which everything I read was really about me. And this mixture of escapism and self-centeredness foreshadowed what was to come shortly thereafter: my descent, which would humble me into a new kind of willingness, a new revelation, and which would lay the groundwork for another chapter of my life.

M Y OBSESSION WITH LITERATURE coincided with another: drugs and alcohol. Novels, like drugs, produced an altered state of consciousness, one in which I felt carried by something beyond myself, toward something unknown, and one which was, to put it simply, pleasurable. In the debates about aesthetics and art, many have said that art's primary goal is essentially the same as drugs' effect: *pleasure*. But anything indulged in inordinately can trap you. The pleasure of what Kierkegaard called "reflection" – reveling in abstract thought and endless *considerations* – quickly becomes habitual indecision. Fantastical, aesthetical impressions can produce pleasure and a sense of possibility at first, but before long they create a state of ambient tension, a static condition composed of many little eschewals and denials. Beauty, lofty feelings, excitement – all turn into pain when used as a means to flee one's existential reality.

Unbound, thinking scatters – unable to cohere – then sours in one's body like curdled milk. That which oppresses us comes from within.

During my fiction-and-drugs phase, everything felt undifferentiated. I had no orienting values, models, or goals that might funnel my energy toward something articulated, concrete, and specific. I wasn't raised religious, or with any clear-cut moral framework. I was weak, prideful, resentful, and so was attracted early on to a way of looking at the world that allowed me to renounce responsibility ad infinitum, and point outward at the world and those around me as the source of my own suffering and failure. Still, I read and read. Despite all evidence to the contrary, I thought that literature might somehow fix me.

Literature's inability to fix my life became apparent when I could not stop doing heroin. My ideas – about how society should be structured; about how thoughts only existed in relation to one another, and thus were all equally arbitrary and self-referential; about my professed moral relativism (but revealed ideological puritanism); about the value of literature being in its *relatability*, and the value of writing being in *expressing oneself* – had no power to effect behavioral change. I could not, by my unaided will, overcome what

I only dimly sensed was something outside my control. I'd wake up in the morning, resolve to not get high, and within an hour I'd be driving to meet my dealer.

I couldn't hold a job and was living at home. My parents had become aware of my condition, and so my mom started keeping her purse beneath her bed. I remember crawling into her bedroom one night as she slept, removing her purse from beneath the bed, and taking twenty of the sixty dollars in her purse. When I got out into the hall I started crying. I didn't want to take the rest – I knew it'd be too obvious, and I'd get caught – but I crawled back into the room and took it anyway. *I did what I did not want to do, and I did not do what I wanted to do.* My habitual evasion of my responsibility to *choose* transformed into something that chose for me. Choices stacked up on one another until they felt like external forces – and by that point, in some sense, they were. It was as if something or someone were directing my limbs, like a puppet's, and no matter how much I tried to *think* my way out of it, I simply couldn't change.

Fleeing the conformity of what I viewed as an arbitrarily oppressive world, I'd flung myself into the service of something much more tyrannical: myself.

I overdosed, went to jail, stole from everyone I came into contact with, lied constantly, and more – all while feeling mysteriously compelled by something I couldn't control. I was free of many things that other people felt oppressed by – jobs, relationships, the pressure to conform in various ways – but I was otherwise enslaved: I'd become a queasy remnant of myself, trapped in pale, cyclical behaviors; I was not free to become who I was.

At the time, I didn't have a language for my problems. I didn't have a way out, only an overwhelming, all-encompassing sense that everything was doomed. I tried to think of ways to fix my life, but my thinking was the problem. I tried to behave differently, but I couldn't. Despite

all that I had read, I had no map to chart a course out of where I'd led myself. And above all I had no power to do so.

I BEGAN TO BECOME who I was meant to be by trying to become another person. Not "another person" in the abstract, but a literal other person whose behavior I emulated, and whose advice I listened to. I met a guy who'd been friends with some of my friends, who'd briefly lived in the house where I spent much of my time writing and getting high, but who'd changed. He told me that if I wanted the kind of life he had, I had to do what he did. It wasn't a matter of "thinking differently," developing more self-knowledge, or having a newfound "resolve"; I simply had to do what other people had done before me, and – I had to take this part on faith – it would work for me too.

At this point, I was desperate. He told me to pray, so I prayed. I didn't expect anything to happen – and nothing did happen. I didn't feel any kind of white light or insight. But I knew that my new friend seemed happy and free. He told me to ask for help in the morning and say thank you at night; the worst-case scenario was that I was talking to a wall. He also told me to stop lying. I couldn't just stop lying right away, but when I lied, I told him, and then I amended the lie. Once, in a conversation with an acquaintance, I said that I worked a certain job I didn't work. Afterward, I called him and confessed that I actually worked construction. His voice sounded like he thought that I was joking, or like he didn't know what to think. I made the phone call feeling terribly embarrassed; I could feel the heat behind my forehead and eyes. But I hung up feeling something I hadn't felt in a long time. I felt free.

The process was slow and arduous. It involved making many small decisions over time. My will and perspective were deformed, so it also involved doing things I did not want to do. I had walked six miles in; now I had to walk six miles out. Part of me resisted. But I had to take responsibility for

myself and stop blaming others. Little by little, I stopped running from the gnawing feelings that emerged when I eschewed responsibility; instead, I limped toward them and, with effort and reluctance, addressed them, often imperfectly and fearfully. Little by little a path was cleared.

By this point, literature played an ambiguous role in my life. I still read, though I didn't know why. I barely wrote. My reasons for writing – essentially solipsistic and therapeutic ones – no longer applied. I began to focus on aesthetics, which worked for a time but eventually felt empty. I slowly chipped away at the crust of self-justification I had built up, and a new kind of possibility was revealed, a new kind of life that was not merely in word or in speech, but in deed and in truth. I found a new mode of being that was active and living.

In order to do this, I had to get comfortable with paradox: freedom in discipline; power in humility; self-esteem in repentance; expansiveness in the apparent narrowness of specific and definite choices. Moreover, I needed models I could imitate in order to develop the capacity for choice. Before, I'd imagined I was fundamentally alone. This was another aspect of reading literature that I enjoyed: just as I could inhabit another consciousness, devoid of existential risk, I could also communicate with others across time in a way that didn't feel oppressive and didn't immediately demand anything of me. But relationships with living people made a claim on me that words on a page did not. I had a responsibility to people in my life, and in coming up against this responsibility – most often in the form of failing to live up to a standard – I learned about myself, and grew.

In recognizing the disharmony between who I was and who I wanted to be, reflected back to me with grace by others, a way forward emerged. But I could not fix myself with myself. I had to look outside of myself, to others, for help. And not just verbal, literary, or philosophical help. I needed to participate, to emulate behaviors I wanted for myself, and then let these behaviors transform my

inner life. Just as certain behaviors like getting high or stealing changed my inner life for the worse, behaviors like helping someone or telling the truth transformed my inner life for the better. I could not think my way into new action, but I could act my way into new thinking. I could not simply read or think a new life into existence. I had to act.

But in order to be able to act, mere moral injunctions and rules didn't work. You will "meet the liberating truth in many forms, except in one form," Paul Tillich writes; "you will never meet it in the form of propositions which you can learn or write down and take home." Human models weren't totally sufficient either. The friend who had initially helped me died. Other friends moved or strayed from the path. My own progress was not straightforwardly linear either – old thinking and behaviors re-emerged in new and cunning forms, requiring more humility or willingness to course-correct – so that my progress was more like an upward spiral than a line. Things could still be

unfathomably dark. The reality of sin and death permeated my life and environment in a way that was ever-present and unavoidable. In these moments, my life became small, and my God became small too. I needed a bigger God.

I was dragged toward this bigger God reluctantly and with much misgiving. My now-wife, Nicolette, became a Christian shortly before we started dating. At church with her mother, she had experienced something she found hard to articulate: the presence of Jesus. I hadn't known many Christians growing up, and still had the typical biases: I could believe in a vague God, but anything beyond that seemed ridiculous, and the manifestations of that belief in culture that I'd been aware of had seemed, if not totally harmful, at least undeniably cringe.

Nicolette's conversion was not, as I'd initially hoped, a phase. While we were dating long distance, in the aftermath of my friend's death, I half-heartedly attempted to go back to my familiar ways, and after I'd gotten sober again I started taking her mom to church as a gesture of goodwill. I hated it, but I went every Sunday. Afterward, her mom would answer questions I had about the sermon, and it all remained essentially impenetrable to me. When I moved, I met some Christians I got along with, and who started a book club that met at my house. We read introductory theology and other books, and they patiently answered my questions and protestations. *What does it mean to "be" a Christian? What could it possibly mean that "Jesus died for our sins"?*

More than any one book or discussion, the act of eating dinner together and hanging out slowly softened me. Christians were people who you could actually *hang out with*. This was a total revelation for me. At one point, a brother from a nearby monastery started coming to our book club and reading the Gospels with us. We would read one Gospel out loud in one sitting, then eat dinner together. He too was someone who

Juan Gris, *Still Life at the Open Window*, 1925.

could hang, a real person with a sense of humor, and who'd considered many of the doubts that I had. Part of this was intellectual: things I'd been reading mapped onto my experiences and observations. I couldn't unsee this, despite a part of me wanting to. Having friends who were Christian, as well as the woman I loved, made me able to *see myself* possibly becoming a Christian.

Jesus doesn't come into a world of self-sufficient automatons, René Girard pointed out. Instead, he enters a world already rife with imitation and says *imitate me.* Imitation had been a crucial aspect of my life, but I had been imitating people who were imperfect, who were themselves imitating imperfect people. There was no grounding here. I needed a transcendent model.

But how could Jesus actually be a model? Love could only be made manifest relationally, and I could not love an abstraction. More, an abstraction could not love me. Through reading the Gospels, long conversations with my wife and friends, praying, and going to church, I began to develop something approximating a relationship with him.

For much of my life, I had labored under the illusion that I could understand everything beforehand, that I could reflect and weigh options and have brilliant thoughts that would then lead me to a certain kind of action – or that could serve as a replacement for action – but a relationship with God, like all relationships, could not be understood beforehand. Before getting married, for example, I could understand all of the potential downsides: the restrictions, the sacrifices, the limitations on my freedom. But I couldn't understand any of the good things beforehand, because the good things were *within the experience itself.* It was the same with my relationship with Jesus. And just as commitment had to precede relationships with people, my relationship with God required a leap of faith in order to participate in it more actively and fully. I decided to submit to that which had been tugging at me for years. Over and against all the fear and hesitation and things I still

did not understand, I got baptized.

Even then a white light did not come over me. The skies didn't open and certainty did not replace the doubt or self-seeking or indecision that had ruled much of my life so far. My relationship to God had to be worked out, with fear and trembling, each day – a stripping away of myself by degrees, a willingness and a hope dependent on my spiritual condition, day by day. But gradually, more grace, conviction, understanding, love, patience, willingness, and perspective entered my life and illuminated it, filling all the nooks and crannies in a way that was both painful and life-giving, making demands on me that both constrained me and set me free.

The mystery of free will – of God being the author of life and of our free participation in his story – is still a mystery. We are characters in God's living, eternal novel – mysteriously free and predestined, alive in love and inclined toward death. Yet we are also mini-authors, made in the image of the author, who blesses our creative capacity and efforts when they are oriented toward life.

Now, literary modes of knowledge and representation continue to deepen my relationship with life and illuminate aspects of it that make my experience richer and more dynamic. I became a novelist myself, after all. But the choiceless consciousness of fiction isn't something I frantically escape into, or merely extract nebulous pleasure from; it's something I engage in with intention, in a way that doesn't ignore life, but rather informs my perspective when I reemerge into a world of deliberative action, and of faith.

God, in his ultimacy, cannot simply be "interpreted" or "read" like a novel. He is not an idea, but rather he is someone who, when I am willing, frees me from the contradicted prison of my will, and points toward a reality beyond this world: one which reaches down into the present, and back into the past, and redeems it; one which – despite my obstinance and hesitation – gives me new life. ➣

# Form and Freedom

*A visual artist, an architect, and a poet describe
the freedom of coloring within the lines.*

IN THE CULTURAL IMAGINATION, the artist is a free spirit. This is perhaps an inheritance from Romanticism, in which the artist stands as the antithesis to the overly rationalistic and capitalistic habits of modernity and the Industrial Revolution. As a result of this, we imagine artists as nonconformists, ruled by intuition and impulse, difficult to pin down, difficult, even, to count on. But the reality for most working artists is a daily life involving a rigor, routine, and precision that we don't typically associate with "free spirits." The musician must master the beat and musical structures of the twelve-bar blues before she can transgress them with the finesse and boldness that epitomizes jazz. The painter tediously prepares canvas and paints to produce a work of visual depth. The dancer's free and graceful movements flow from decades of disciplined training and daily repetition of technique.

Below, three artists from different disciplines reflect on the interplay between freedom and structure in their work. Far from inhibiting freedom, these artists find that it is often through accepting formal limitations, structure, and routine that their practice can become intuitive and free-flowing. —*Joy Marie Clarkson*

## The Discipline of Egg Tempera
### Hannah Rose Thomas

In the painting process, there is a subtle balance between structure and creative freedom, discipline and spontaneity. I am especially conscious of this tension in the traditional painting methods I use. My portrait paintings are rooted in the symbolism and painting techniques used in Byzantine iconography and the early Renaissance, and yet they address contemporary themes such

Hannah Rose Thomas, *Islamic architecture reflects the purity
and calm elsewhere found in nature,* photograph with filter, 2016.

as forced displacement, religious and ethnic persecution, and sexual violence in conflict. While the subject matter is contemporary, traditional techniques and an attentive, prayerful approach remain at the heart of these paintings.

I tend to work in egg tempera, which is a beautiful medium that requires a methodical, disciplined, and craftsman-like approach. Freedom can be found within discipline and limitations. While it may seem paradoxical, discipline provides the structure, consistency, and concentrated focus for creativity to flourish.

I begin the day preparing the natural pigments by hand and mixing them with the natural binder, egg yolk. This helps still my mind and heart before I start painting. It is a meditative process that cultivates a ritual preparedness, an invitation to attendance and reverence. Tempera can only be applied in thin, translucent layers, and it has a very fast drying time. Therefore, it takes innumerable layers of paint to build up the finished portrait. I begin by modeling shadow, then light, for the tonal underpainting in verdaccio before adding glazes of color. It is a process that cannot be rushed; any attempts to apply thicker paint layers make it difficult to achieve harmonious tonal transitions. This makes tempera a less spontaneous medium than oil paint. However, the jewel-like luminosity of color and the depth of presence in an egg tempera painting is a mystery that emerges through the rich beauty of the layering process.

The repetitive brushstrokes of translucent paint require patient attention. For the British novelist and philosopher Iris Murdoch, art "demands moral effort and teaches quiet attention." Murdoch elevates attention as integral to the moral and ethical life. Likewise, the painstaking egg tempera methods of the early Renaissance,

*Hannah Rose Thomas is a British artist, human rights activist, and the author of* Plough's 2024 title *Tears of Gold.*

Hannah Rose Thomas, *Maria and Nadiia,*
portrait work in progress, egg tempera on panel, 2022.

and, in some of the paintings, the use of gold leaf, is integral to my ethics and aesthetics. These techniques are how I seek to respond to, honor, and revere the stories that I have heard. The theologian Rowan Williams highlights the importance of the "reverence, patience, time-taking between agents in creation" that demands an "awareness of the impenetrable mysteriousness of the other's hinterland and gratitude for life-giving."

To create is an act of faith. It is to persevere in the hope that the elusive "impenetrable mysteriousness" of the other will shimmer through the layers of paint. In the painting process there is a delicate balance between a perfectionist drive for artistic mastery and a humble searching and receptive openness, a vulnerability before the unknown.

## Architecture's Crisis of Freedom
Charles Howell

The most formative technological advancement for building design was the production of steel. Sir Henry Bessemer developed efficient means for the alloy's production in the middle of the nineteenth century. And it was not long after, in the 1880s, that Burnham and Root architects completed the Rand-McNally building in Chicago – the first all-steel framed skyscraper. Bessemer's innovation took on new forms as further advancement in construction materials continued throughout the twentieth century. From reinforced concrete to lightweight alloys, architecture became proof of the Enlightenment's claims to advancement.

Since the inauguration of culture, buildings were historically constrained to the statical limitations of their materials. A building could only be as tall as the base layer of stones could support. Its openings only as wide as the integrity of its arches. Its span only as great as its columns could withstand. The classical orders were mathematically precise formulas to ensure the structural stability and public safety of buildings. The Greeks were just as concerned with physics as they were with aesthetics.

All of this changed with steel. Architecture was liberated from its natural limitations. And as such, the art of architecture was presented with

---

*In modern architecture, the question of freedom was never really one of unbridled spontaneity but always one of what to do with the limited capacity of freedom.*

---

an identity crisis. What norms should govern this newfound freedom? What does this freedom mean for humanity's relationship to nature?

Modern architecture took form as an attempt to answer this question. German-American architect Ludwig Mies van der Rohe, representing one position, sought to fully embrace the novel possibilities of buildings, in order to establish a new connection with nature. He saw that modern materials could erase the stringent dichotomy of inside-outside in buildings. Beginning with his Pavilion in Barcelona (1929) and perhaps perfected in his Farnsworth House outside Chicago (1946–51), he used steel to span entire lengths of a structure, infilling its frame wholly with glass. To be in these buildings was to be in immediate sight of what lay outside. It was to be protected, but never fully detached from nature. American architect Frank Lloyd Wright, taking another position, strove to reflect the aesthetics of nature through structural innovations. Not only does his Prairie style utilize the materials local to the site,

---

*Charles Howell is an architect. He received his PhD from the University of St Andrews, Scotland.*

he also realized buildings could reflect the natural topology. Fallingwater is an exquisite example, as it mimics the shape of its mountainous setting.

These modernists reveal that even with techno-logical innovation humans are always tethered to the natural realm. Their design approaches, in fact, attempt to honor this relationship. But they only see such honor as valid if it happens in congruency with the historical moment. The retrieval move-ments of premodern architecture – neoclassical, neo-Gothic, etc. – are, structurally, farces. Supported by steel, their façades are nostalgic whimpers. Their appearances hide their modern essence.

In modern architecture, the question of freedom was never really one of unbridled spontaneity but always one of what to do with the limited capacity of freedom. Undoubtedly, the emphasis is slightly tilted to the former aspect. But the deep reality of the natural world will never completely loosen its grasp. Architecture is forced to recognize this limitation, and thus, can serve as a reminder to our more abstract musings on freedom.

### *Reflections on the Sonnet*
Malcolm Guite

I have found that in the composition of sonnets the form itself, far from constraining me, gives me freedom. It enables me to say things with a power, a concentration, a fully embodied form, that a freer and perhaps more rambling exercise in *vers libre* could not attain. This paradox, that we find freedom through form, has been frequently attested and indeed explored by poets who have chosen to write in form, particularly in the

---

*Malcolm Guite is a priest, poet, singer-songwriter, and the author of several books.*

Frank Lloyd Wright, *Fallingwater*, color pencil on tracing paper, 1935.

sonnet form. Samuel Daniel, the Elizabethan and Jacobean poet who wrote a sonnet sequence called *Delia*, puts it very well in his *A Defence of Ryme*: "Ryme is no impediment to his conceit, rather giues him wings to mount and carries him, not out of his course, but as it were beyond his power to a farre happier flight."

Time and again I have had this experience of being carried "beyond my power" to "a far happier flight." Something far more generative, more creative, is drawn from me in the very exercise of keeping to my self-imposed boundaries. The "bounding line," as William Blake called it, is, in the very act of setting a boundary, concentrating the energy of the poem, like the banks of a river channeling the current that might otherwise dissipate in a tepid lake. The poet in *Timon of Athens* says poetry is "a current [which] flies each bound it chafes." The very effort to channel it is what gives the current force, and of course the "bound," the end of the line, or the turn of the sonnet can sometimes be overrun to great effect – the poem can fly the bound. Yet even that freedom to play with and stretch the rule is not an effect one can achieve without the self-imposed rule.

But there is much more at stake here than literary style. In making these choices we are ultimately concerned with beauty, truth, and goodness. The first reason for choosing the sonnet form is beauty – it is a beautiful form in itself, as Daniel also emphasizes in the same work quoted above: "Euery language hath her proper number or measure fitted to vse and delight, which . . . by the allowance of the Eare, doth indenize, and make naturall. All verse is but a frame of wordes confinde within certaine measure; differing from the ordinarie speach, and introduced, the better to expresse mens conceipts, both for delight and memorie." There are beauties, attractions for both the "eare" and the eye that are unique to the sonnet form. As the contemporary poet Don Paterson puts it in his introduction to his anthology *101 Sonnets: From Shakespeare to Heaney*, "It presents both poet and reader with a vivid symmetry that is the perfect emblem of the meaning a sonnet seeks to embody . . . so a sonnet is a paradox, a little squared circle, a mandala that invites our meditation."

And what of goodness and truth? Here I have a deeper reason yet for employing the sonnet form. For me it is an act of countercultural resistance. Since the Enlightenment our culture has been besotted with the notion of autonomy, of self-rule, of the isolated will of the individual trumping every other consideration. But in earlier ages, and in my own Christian faith, I find there is a deeper truth at work: that to live from and in obedience to God, who is the sum of all good, is in fact to become free and happy in a way that no amount of self-dictation and private wish fulfillment could approach. It is indeed true that "his service is perfect freedom." I think of myself, my own life, not as an arbitrary piece of self-expression, but as a poem that is still being spoken by my Creator. He has chosen a particular form for me as a poem. He has set my bounding lines and in keeping to those lines I not only exercise my creativity, but I become more truly myself; I acquire form and coherence. When I tried to express that some years ago, the best form was, naturally, a sonnet:

## O Sapientia

I cannot think unless I have been thought,
Nor can I speak unless I have been spoken.
I cannot teach except as I am taught,
Or break the bread except as I am broken.
O Mind behind the mind through which I seek,
O Light within the light by which I see,
O Word beneath the words with which I speak,
O founding, unfound Wisdom, finding me,
O sounding Song whose depth is sounding me,
O Memory of time, reminding me,
My Ground of Being, always grounding me,
My Maker's Bounding Line, defining me,
  Come, hidden Wisdom, come with all you bring,
  Come to me now, disguised as everything.

Poem from *Sounding the Seasons* (Canterbury Press, 2012).

# "Paraguayans Don't Read"

*In a dictatorship, literature can nurture freedom.*
*In a democracy, does it matter?*

**SANTIAGO RAMOS**

I<small>T'S AN ORDINARY PORTRAIT</small> of a man wearing a duckbill beret, a small piece of luggage in each hand, and he's leaving. You wouldn't think it's a portrait. It looks like a picture you took by mistake, or a figure in the background of somebody else's picture. In fact, that man has his back to the camera. He's facing left, like he's looking before crossing the street. He is walking across a concrete esplanade, and beyond him are an electrical tower, a patch of grass, a blurry sign, and a brick wall.

It is one of the most famous photographs in the history of a small nation.

Augusto Roa Bastos is considered, by wide consensus, to be the greatest writer that the Republic of Paraguay has ever produced. "Roa Bastos was Paraguay's entry into universal literature," a child might hear in school. He is that man, off in the distance, his back to the camera, walking and looking around. He's probably nervous in the photograph, because he has just been told by agents of the dictator to leave the country. The concrete esplanade is part of the border crossing that connects with the Argentine city of Clorinda, across the river from the Paraguayan capital of Asunción. He is about to begin a period of exile that will last for eight years.

In fact, this will not be Roa Bastos's first exile. At age thirty, he had fled the country after the failed revolution of 1947, which tried to overthrow the eight-year dictatorship of General Higinio Morínigo. Hundreds of revolutionaries had crossed the border to avoid arrest or execution. Roa Bastos went to Buenos Aires and eventually settled in France.

I CAME ACROSS THIS PHOTO this past summer in Asunción, while I was spending a month with family, in the place I was born. There, I read Roa Bastos's autobiographical novel, *The Prosecutor*, about the life of a political exile who plots to assassinate the dictator who exiled him. And while I was there, I visited bookstores in search of another book: my great-uncle's memoirs of the 1947 revolution.

Like Roa Bastos, Colonel Alfredo Ramos participated in the 1947 revolution. He had fought in the successful war against Bolivia, between 1932 and 1935. In 1947, he was summoned by a military faction stationed in the northern city of Concepción, where he was asked to join the revolt against Higinio Morínigo. Ramos analyzed the situation and concluded that the revolt had a small chance of success. He said no. But the next day, after the faction succeeded in taking Concepción, he was summoned once again, and this time the colonel accepted. He led the revolutionaries in a key battle in the town of Tacuatí, and was promoted to the rank of brigadier general. The revolution did not succeed, which is why the cover of his memoir, *Concepción 1947*, refers to his pre-revolutionary rank; he would die a colonel. Like Roa Bastos, the colonel escaped: he crossed the border into Brazil and then settled in Buenos Aires, Argentina.

*Concepción 1947* is hard to find. I remember seeing it around the house as a kid in Asunción. But several moves later, it was nowhere to be found in my parents' home in the United States. I remember the glossy cover – it must have been printed in the 1980s or '90s. As far as I can tell, the book's publisher no longer exists. None of the bookstores could find the title in their inventory. I don't trust the computer information systems in Paraguay, so I made sure to visit several stores from the biggest corporate chain – El Lector – but found nothing. It didn't occur to me to check used book stores until a week into my search.

"PARAGUAYANS DON'T READ" is a refrain I had heard since I was a child. Official statistics estimate that the average Paraguayan reads 0.25 books per year. I do not blame Paraguay for this. A founding father and first dictator of the nation, Dr. José Gaspar Rodríguez de Francia closed the Catholic seminary and discouraged higher education generally. Even though de Francia was a man of the Enlightenment, a lapsed Catholic, and a reader of Voltaire, he made sure that literature was censored in the nascent republic.

Subsequent dictators followed suit: they ruled by treating the people as illiterate children. Where would the used books come from? Who would have used them? The only used book store in Asunción that I knew about,

---

*Santiago Ramos is the executive editor of the* Wisdom of Crowds *Substack and a longtime contributor at* Commonweal. *He is also a* Plough *contributing editor.*

the once-famous Comuneros bookstore downtown, had closed years before. To my surprise, Google Maps was able to find several others in the city. On a Sunday afternoon, I walked to one of them.

The professional signage at the front door was the only indication that I was entering a place of business, but it was really a house – in fact, somebody's home. Today, Asunción is a city of high-rises and shopping malls; the houses of the wealthy are surrounded by brick walls or electrified fences. This little house was from an earlier time. A maze of bookshelves of varying height and length carved out random spaces under the high colonial ceiling. Above, on the roof, the weather had turned the aged, orange earthenware tiles black and green. Below, the air was thick with dust and mildew. It was an old house, and an old man was living in it. He had two assistants. One was manning a small register perched on a tall wooden table. Another was rummaging around the store, his neck long and arched forward, as if before a book. He looked at me suspiciously both times I came to the store. I believe he was the son of the owner of the store, the old man who sat on a chair, several books resting on the half-globe of his abdomen. He stood up when I arrived. Not too many people must visit the store on Sundays. Then he started asking me questions. Asunción is a small town, and most people have one or two

degrees of separation from each other.

"Where do you come from?" You can ask probing questions in Paraguay without sounding rude. After a brief exchange, he had enough data to announce: "I know your father. I sold him books."

Don Brabant, as the old man was called, was a bookseller by vocation. He was also a courageous man. While my father was a high-school and university student in the 1970s, when books were harder to come by, Don Brabant was his go-to guy. More importantly, the seventies were the time of the worst repression by the government of General Stroessner. This was the decade of Operation Condor: the CIA-backed coordinated effort by the secret police of Chile, Argentina, Uruguay, and Paraguay to root out all leftist elements, real or imagined, in southern South America. These efforts succeeded, but not without disappearing thousands of people and torturing and incarcerating many more. During this time, Roa Bastos and many other writers either fled the continent or lived in fear.

I now had two requests for Don Brabant. First, do you have a copy of Colonel Alfredo Ramos's memoirs about the revolution, *Concepción 1947*? Second, I am a journalist: may I interview you about what it was like to be a bookseller during the dictatorship of Alfredo Stroessner?

In response to the first request, Don Brabant began combing his bookshelves, looking up and down, pointing at the extreme top and bottom of several shelves so his son, the silent swan-necked man who had stared at me since I entered the place, could reach for books he suspected might be what I was looking for, but he could not find it. "I know the book," he told me, and soon enough, the man showed me a picture of the book on his cellphone. "I don't think we have it here – I thought we had it here," said Don

Brabant. He found another book about the 1947 revolution, and several books by a historian named Ramos, who was not the colonel. "I will find it and let you know on WhatsApp. When you come to pick it up, we can do the interview."

The man at the register added, "We will find the book. Don Brabant has done interviews for the radio before."

In *The Prosecutor,* Roa Bastos has his exiled protagonist wonder whether books were being written in Latin American nations under dictatorship. His best bet, he thinks, is to dream them into being:

> I knew nothing of what was currently being written in Latin American countries, most of which were subject to dictatorships, persecutions, and repressions of all kinds. Their cultures of resistance, struggling to survive, could do little for an art and a literature that served only as entertainment for girls from the well-off classes. They had no immediate practical use. They did not exist. I invented those books by contemporary authors that I was obliged to read, but that I would probably never read, and that would never be written. Some names, some books, reached me. I did not know who they were. I did not touch those books that stank of internal exile, of repressive suffocation.

In fact, writers and artists flourished during the Stroessner era. Today those same writers are largely forgotten outside a small circle of devoted readers. The liberal José Luis Appleyard wrote modernist poetry while making a living as a newspaper editor. Elvio Romero, a great communist poet, wrote from exile. Josefina Plá wrote histories and fiction, becoming (among other things) the great historian-critic of Paraguayan letters. Carlos Colombino painted abstract, neo-cubist renderings of the faces of power – of the general himself, even. Magazines mattered, ideas mattered, even poetry mattered – at least in Asunción, where a higher literacy rate than the rest of the country and relative freedom of communication allowed culture to flourish. This is why the prospect of an interview with Don Brabant became more exciting for me than finding my great-uncle's memoirs. What is another war book compared to an interview with a humble servant of the Republic of Letters, whose silent sacrifices and fearful trade nurtured the minds of intellectuals

---

## What is another war book compared to an interview with a humble servant of the Republic of Letters?

---

during the darkest days of a thirty-four-year-long military dictatorship?

I heard a story from my father which, to me, encapsulated the absurd little regime of the 1970s. It is March 1970 or '71, the end of summer, and students everywhere are starting their semester. The Catholic University of Paraguay sits next to the cathedral, separated by a narrow passageway. In front of the university and cathedral is a vast plaza, and adjacent to these is the Paraguay River. It is humid and hot. Nine students assemble in a classroom with high ceilings, three ceiling fans, and tall open windows. The professor enters and writes his name on the board. The course is a seminar on the philosophy of religion, or modern philosophy (the narrator, my father, can't remember).

The professor and the students discuss the readings for the seminar. The Catholic University of Paraguay is, at that time, one of two institutions of higher learning in Paraguay, the other being the National University. The dictatorship controls the National University, but the Catholic one maintains a modicum of independence from the regime. The professor assigns a book by British philosopher Bertrand Russell: *Why I Am Not a Christian.*

Like most works of European philosophy, at least ones from the twentieth century, Russell's book is not available in Asunción, a city of less than a million people, relatively isolated from the other great cities of the region. (Roa Bastos described the landlocked state of Paraguay as "an island surrounded by land.") So how could they get the book? One student says he is making

---

The professor surveys the classroom. He squints. "I think our students are getting arrested," he says. And it so happens that they are.

---

a trip over the weekend to Buenos Aires – a much bigger city, connected to the rest of the world by the Atlantic Ocean – and that he might be able to pick up ten copies for the class.

A week passes and the class meets again. The student isn't there. The professor asks his students if they know where he might be. No one has heard from or seen him since before he left for Buenos Aires. Oh well, he must be sick or something. Another student, Pablo, let's call him, says that he will look for him after class.

Another week passes, and the student is still nowhere to be seen, and Pablo is gone now too.

Strange. But these were times when people could not be reached easily as they are today. Not everyone had a telephone. If someone went out of town for something, you would not hear from them before they returned home. Class carried on with other readings and discussions.

The following week, neither the first missing student nor Pablo shows up. And now a third student is missing.

The professor surveys the classroom. He squints. "I think our students are getting arrested," he says. And it so happens that they are. The professor talks to the dean of students, who contacts the archbishop of Asunción. The archbishop pays a visit to the chief of police who, at first, does not want to release the students. Why would the archbishop defend students who are smuggling a book titled *Why I Am Not a Christian*? Does he not know what happens to priests in Cuba? Is this archbishop in fact a communist? A follower of liberation theology? But eventually he lets the students go, and the semester continues without another incident.

I ENTERED DON BRABANT'S BOOKSHOP with great excitement. An interview that would serve as a soliloquy in the great drama of life under the dictatorship. The tender rose of liberty under the bookseller's cupped hand, during a rainstorm. The fire of liberty, never burning more brightly than when threatened by the policeman's water cannon. I would be the humble scribe.

Don Brabant asked for a couch to be brought for me. I sat before him. The assistant stood next to Don Brabant, examining me. I started asking him about his work with Don Brabant. "What do you enjoy reading?" I asked him.

"Paraguayan history . . . the Chaco War. Triple Alliance." Terse replies.

"I distributed the World Literature series to the major high schools," Don Brabant explains, "Christ the King, the International School, San José. The major literary academies. I was a young man. I got into this business through friends. I was not linked to the political side of things. It was another time. I was involved in the book business."

"During this time – the 1970s – there were a lot of protests," I offered.

"Yes, a lot of protests. Very violent." The old man looked up at the assistant. Before he said anything, the man at the cashier piped in: "Bring some cornbread and beer." The assistant did as he was told, but while he was away in the kitchen, the old man added that he preferred rum.

"Was the book business dangerous?"

"It had its dangers."

"Was there censorship?"

"Some books were explicitly banned, yes. *Paloma Blanca Paloma Negra* [white dove, black dove]. Books by Elvio Romero and Rubén Bareiro Saguier."

"My grandfather has a vinyl album by Atahualpa Yupanqui. He was a communist. I asked him, 'How did you buy that in Paraguay? It was printed in the 1970s.' And he said, 'I went to the store.'"

"Yes, there were many books you could get."

"Even Herbert Marcuse's books? I saw Marcuse on his bookshelf."

"Yes. Books by Marx or Lenin were banned. But you could get Marcuse."

"Where?"

"In a bookstore. There were bookstores."

At this point the cashier was at the liquor store and he called the assistant, who was sitting next to Don Brabant. "He wants to know what kind?"

"Peach rum. Peach."

A minute later another call: "They are out of peach."

"They have peach everywhere."

"They're out, he says."

"Passionfruit then." The old man turned toward me. "There was censorship that was half-hearted and ambiguous."

"Do you think it's ironic that people read more and writers were more important during the dictatorship than after 1989, when democracy came?"

"There were more cultural events back then for sure."

"In a strange way," I was fishing for a quote here, "was it better back then, to be a writer, I mean?"

"Some things were better and some things were worse." The rum arrived. The three of us drank for the next few hours, pacifying my frustration at the lack of drama I had uncovered.

If Don Brabant's life, as he told it, was lacking in dramatic material, Roa Bastos's had more than enough. Exiled in Buenos Aires during the 1960s, Bastos made his name as a writer with a collection of stories, *Thunder Among the Leaves*, and a novel, *Son of Man*. In 1974, he published his masterpiece: *I, the Supreme*. The novel is a portrait of the nineteenth-century dictator José Gaspar Rodríguez de Francia. The critics called it a postmodern historical novel that blended historical documents and narrative fiction. General Alfredo Stroessner, who was the dictator of Paraguay at the time of the book's publication, believed it to be about himself – that is, a thinly veiled critique of his own regime.

Why did Bastos get kicked out of Paraguay in 1982? There was no official judicial process through which he lost his passport and citizenship. The decision was taken by the dictator himself. General Stroessner already knew about Bastos. No doubt *I, the Supreme* factored into his decision. So did a few columns Bastos had written in an Argentine newspaper, critical of his regime. The ambiguity that Don Brabant had talked about played out to Bastos's detriment. He had returned to Paraguay thinking his exile was over. He wanted to register his newborn son as a Paraguayan citizen, and that was something you were legally required to return to Paraguay to do. No sooner did the last exile end than a new one began.

But most of the stories of censorship and persecution are low-key, banal. A friend of my father's freaked out when, as a kid, he left a copy of Che Guevara's memoirs in the bottom of a trunk, which was about to go through customs. (The policeman missed it.) My uncle wondered why so-and-so could get away with playing leftist songs in public, on his guitar after school. (The kid was well-connected in the government.) Don Brabant was right: in the ambiguity of unfreedom, only the courageous or the clever could navigate.

But Don Brabant himself could not supply me with even a minor censorship tale. Eventually, two rums deep, we talked about Paraguayan history – the default topic of all bookworms in the country. I looked around: most of the books around me were histories. A big chunk of those histories, in turn, were military memoirs or narratives of war. Lots of lists of names of who did or did not participate in this or that battle. Histories or – I slowly noticed – rows and rows of copies of the civil code. Law books. Law students would always make good customers. Red or blue, drab, binders of civil codes and photocopies of civil codes. And it slowly dawned on me that almost every single book around me had been published in Paraguay. Almost nothing from Argentina or

Mexico or Spain. Everything was Paraguayan and at least a quarter of a century old. This was less a bookstore than a time capsule. No book seemed younger than the country's democracy, and no one born under democratic rule seemed to have any need for books.

Sadly, one book was nowhere to be found: my great-uncle's memoirs. The cashier broke the news. "We can't find the book," he told us. "I looked for it everywhere. I think I know where I can get a copy, but it is out of town. I will let you know."

A FEW DAYS LATER, I got a call from the assistant. They had the book. They offered to deliver it to me. I told them I would pick it up myself the next day, as I had to travel to that part of town.

Shortly after the liberation of France in World War II, the philosopher Jean-Paul Sartre wrote in *The Atlantic Monthly*:

Never were we freer than under the German occupation. . . . The more the Nazi venom crept into our thoughts the more each precise thought became a conquest. The more the omnipotent police tried to enforce our silence, the more each of our words became a precious declaration of principle. The more we were pursued, the more each one of our gestures took on the nature of an engagement. The frequently atrocious circumstances of our struggle made us at the same time live – without any deceit, nakedly, in this torn and untenable situation which one calls the state of man. Exile, captivity, above all, death, which one easily shies from during happier times, were then our perpetual worry, and we were to learn that they were not avoidable accidents, not even constant or objective threats, but that we must discover in them our lot, our fate, the deepest source of our being.

Writers living in a democracy are not so lucky. They have to deal with penury and apathy. Sometimes, floods. The day I was supposed to pick up the book, I called ahead of time, because it was raining. Asunción lacks proper drainage infrastructure; the place floods every time it storms. The bookstore, being in a low corner of town, got inundated with six inches of water that had accumulated in the blind alley in front of the house. "Don't come today, it's a mess," the cashier told me in a voice memo.

I was annoyed. A city needs infrastructure. Why can't I have my book? I thought about that passage from Sartre, and about the famous Roa Bastos photo. The story of crossing customs with ten copies of Bertrand Russell, or one stray copy of Che Guevara's *Motorcycle Diaries*. Could it be that these people all lived in a reality where the very act of writing carried a weight and meaning lacking in our own time? Was it fair to compare our boredom and apathy with their suffering? But I was enjoying the very freedom that they suffered for and wrote about. So what is writing for?

Perhaps Don Brabant's book collection reflected his own particular tastes, or his niche in the market. The dozen locales of El Lector throughout the city – many more stores than an American city the size of Asunción would have – carried books from other Latin American countries, and Europe. Maybe the reading habits of the people around me were richer than I was judging them to be.

Or maybe there was something about art and literature that made it the fitting way to oppose dictatorship and nurture freedom. If you want to think freely but you're surrounded by informants, it is not a bad idea to do so on the page, in meter and rhyme, or telling a story, or painting a picture. The dictatorship can't reach into the paper while it sits between you and the desk. But the Paraguay of the post-dictatorship era of economic growth and democracy has a new center of power. I do not know what it is; I know it by its fruits. It is not a general. It is not even a person. The Colorado Party – Stroessner's party – still runs the government. It still wins elections. But they are in charge of the state, not

> If you want to think freely but you're surrounded by informants, it is not a bad idea to do so on the page, in meter and rhyme, or telling a story, or painting a picture.

of the destiny of the nation as a whole, which appears to be carried by a strange current.

Those who lived under Stroessner did not grow up with high-rises, glamorous shopping centers, McDonald's franchises, highways, or the Southern Cone Common Market trade agreement with Argentina, Brazil, Uruguay, and Chile, which would facilitate economic growth and labor mobility. I remember once talking about the lack of good public education in Paraguay with an uncle. "It is a disgrace, the quality of public schools in the interior of the country," he said.

"Yeah . . . you know, every Paraguayan kid has a human right to read *Don Quixote*."

"What are you talking about?" he said. "They need computers. They need math."

I thought about my great-uncle, Colonel Ramos, writing his memoirs in exile, his revolution a failure, and his life saved by a lucky, timely plane ride out of the country.

The day after the rain, the sky was blue, but Colonel Ramos's book was lost again. The cashier called: "I don't know what happened to it." ⬧

# The Story of Freedom

*Freedom can't be neatly defined. Instead,*
*the Bible presents it as a history.*

**HEINRICH ARNOLD**

FREEDOM: A GLORIOUS and tantalizing word, universally loved, sought after, sloganized, sung about, and fought over. But when was the last time any of us paused to think through what it means? Is it a right, a gift, a choice, a responsibility, a conquest?

Most definitions of freedom focus on what the Russian-British philosopher Isaiah Berlin referred to as "negative liberty": we are free when no one and nothing is constraining or coercing us. No one is preventing us from doing what we want, and there is no physical law that restricts

J. Kirk Richards, *New England Reverie*, oil, 2023.

us. Considerations of this kind of freedom often focus on gaining freedom in liberation from slavery or restraint.

Thoughts of freedom draw us to nature – we think of the freedom of a soaring bird, the freedom of escaping to a mountain wilderness, with all its sights, smells, and sounds: the natural wonders of God's creation. It's a beautiful picture of a form of freedom. But is it the best expression of the freedom God intends for us? Yes, birds can fly, nature seems carefree, but animals and natural phenomena are equally bound to harsh cycles of cause and effect, food chains, and the universal laws of nature.

Is freedom the same thing as technical power, power over creation? Marvels of science and engineering conjure a kind of freedom – we harness water, wind, and fuel for electricity, telecommunication, flight, space exploration, computing networks, and most recently AI. But too often our technical power leads to a kind of slavery: we become addicted to our devices. If we outsource too many tasks, and even creative endeavors, to our technology, aren't we in danger of losing our own ability to do those tasks ourselves, and thus of limiting our freedom even as we think we are expanding it?

Others think of political power: for instance, the great American experiment of a free republic. We certainly enjoy many protected freedoms, and those who wrote the Constitution were inspired by the ideal of freedom, which we are still fumbling to grasp. Yet freedom gained from political power is fragile and limited: all governments struggle to align their laws with true justice; all politicians are subject to the corrupting power of money.

Power and freedom, then, are related. But they are not the same.

Negative liberty, "freedom *from*," is important. So, too, is freedom in terms of political rights.

But what Berlin called "positive liberty" is equally important. This "freedom *to*" is our internal power to act – to act according to reason and according to the good. This kind of freedom has been called virtue. Yet even this does not fully illuminate the nature of freedom.

IT'S TIME TO TURN to the Bible. "It is for freedom that Christ has set us free," the apostle Paul writes (Gal. 5:1). This statement almost deifies freedom – Jesus sets us free for freedom. What is this freedom that seems to be an end in itself? We know that we are made for God himself. And therefore this freedom – the freedom that Paul describes – must be an aspect of God's nature, and because of that, an integral part of his design for humanity bearing his image. Paul continues, admonishing the Galatians to "stand firm . . . and do not let yourselves be burdened again by a yoke of slavery."

Freedom from slavery is the story of God's chosen people. "Let my people go" formed a new nation devoted to God (Exod. 5:1). With vivid, dramatic instructions, God used Moses to lead his people out of slavery in Egypt and into a new life as a free people. He wanted to relate to his people in freedom, so he set them free.

Being set free from external slavery is only the beginning, though. Freedom demands that we make choices. And the freedom that God wants for his people is their voluntary allegiance. More than voluntary: he wants our delighted and loving allegiance, trusting in his goodness and being true to the spirit of his commands. It is for this relationship that he gave us free will.

The opening of the Book of Genesis shows that God created us to do his work in freedom rather than out of blind compulsion or even as the irrational animals do. This is the picture we get when God blessed the man and woman and

---

*Heinrich Arnold serves as a senior pastor for the Bruderhof in the United States and abroad. He lives with his wife and family at the Woodcrest Bruderhof.*

that was its name" (Gen. 2:19).

But true freedom is not limitless. Just because we have free will does not mean that everything that we will is good. Indeed, the reason we have wills is so that they might be aligned with the good, with God's own will.

But sometimes, we desire to call good what we want: to take to ourselves the power of naming not just animals, but right and wrong. And right and wrong are not subject to our wills. That paradox pops into focus right in the beginning of the story of Adam and Eve: "The Lord God took the man and put him in the garden of Eden to till it and keep it. And the Lord God commanded the man, 'You may freely eat of every tree of the garden; but of the tree of the knowledge of good and evil you shall not eat, for in the day that you eat of it you shall die.'" (Gen. 2:15–17).

Our ancestors knew the boundary God had set, but they were still free to break it, and they did: "So when the woman saw that the tree was good for food, and that it was a delight to the eyes, and that the tree was to be desired to make one wise, she took of its fruit and ate, and she also gave some to her husband who was with her, and he ate" (Gen. 3:6).

Even after they were banished, Adam still had his task of choosing, his task of cultivating, his task of naming: "The man named his wife Eve, because she was the mother of all living" (Gen. 3:20).

And God, who gave Adam and Eve full freedom – even the freedom to turn away from him – saw down through deep time to the end of his plan, and responded in love, with an act of loving service that anticipated the sacrifice that would one day make a way for Adam and Eve's sons and daughters to return to him: "And the Lord God made garments of skins for the man

charged them to "be fruitful and multiply, and fill the earth and subdue it, and have dominion over the fish of the sea and over the birds of the air and over every living thing that moves upon the earth" (Gen. 1:28).

Our original task is one of freedom – we are free to eat of "every plant yielding seed that is upon the face of all the earth, and every tree with seed in its fruit" (Gen. 1:29). We are free, and that freedom is integral to our task. God gave Adam authority and a corresponding freedom in his first job, to name every living creature: "So out of the ground the Lord God formed every animal of the field and every bird of the air, and brought them to the man to see what he would call them; and whatever the man called every living creature,

J. Kirk Richards, *Consider the Lilies*, oil, 2023.

and for his wife, and clothed them" (Gen. 3:21).

This story in itself shows that freedom – the power to choose freely and to act freely, and the importance of using that power in accord with the good – is integral to God's plan for us as his people.

In the Bible, as in our own time, there is a political aspect to the question of freedom. The freedom of God's people is a freedom in covenant: a treaty of mutual self-binding that comes with responsibilities.

Thus the covenant between Abraham and God is built on the ideal of freedom. In Genesis 17:2, God says, "I will make my covenant between me and you." Covenants demand action from both sides. They are not just contracts, but mutual gifts of self. That is why God continually encourages personal, willing participation in the covenant.

There are many examples of this. Right from the beginning, leaders of the tribes and of the smaller groups are freely chosen, not mandated (Deut. 1:13). At every turn, obedience to the command-ments involves a free choice, not compulsion. Moses urges the people to choose to do God's will (Deut. 30:19), and Joshua urges the people to make the same choice. This freedom is, we are told, not absolute independence, but rather a freedom of service: "If it is evil in your eyes to serve the Lord, choose this day whom you will serve, whether the gods your fathers served in the region beyond the River, or the gods of the Amorites in whose land you dwell. But as for me and my house, we will serve the Lord" (Josh. 24:15).

The wisdom literature deepens this under-standing: we are to "choose" the right way (Ps. 25:12) and "choose" the fear of the Lord (Prov. 1:29). Further, we have the power to reject violence and evil of our own volition (Prov. 3:31). But continuing to make bad choices, this literature reveals, also has a negative impact on the will: the will is weakened as it keeps returning to what has ensnared it before (Prov. 5:22). It is this tendency of the will to enslavement, this tendency of

humans to return to slavery, that God has a long-term plan to address.

Thus it is no surprise that the concept of freedom is woven throughout the prophecies about Jesus. In Isaiah's prophecy about a young leader, the boy's power to choose between evil and good is the mark of the coming victory against the kings who oppose Israel (Isa. 7:15). And it is Isaiah, too, who declares what that victory will look like: "The Spirit of the Sovereign Lord is on me," he writes in his own voice, which is also the voice of one who is to come, "because the Lord has anointed me to proclaim good news to the poor. He has sent me to bind up the brokenhearted, to proclaim freedom for the captives and release from darkness for the prisoners" (Isa. 61:1).

FOR PAUL, freedom was one of the most important aspects of what it means to follow Jesus and be part of the people of God. In his Letter to the Romans he makes the point that it is not only human beings but all of creation that will be made free with the victory of Christ: "For the creation was subjected to futility, not of its own will but by the will of the one who subjected it, in hope that the creation itself will be set free from its bondage to decay and will obtain the freedom of the glory of the children of God" (Rom. 8:20–21).

When God is there, he brings freedom: "When-ever anyone turns to the Lord, the veil is taken away. Now the Lord is the Spirit, and where the Spirit of the Lord is, there is freedom. And we all, who with unveiled faces contemplate the Lord's glory, are being transformed into his image with ever-increasing glory, which comes from the Lord, who is the Spirit" (2 Cor. 3:16–18).

Of all the books in the New Testament, Gala-tians mentions freedom the most. The motif of slavery and freedom runs throughout the letter. In the beginning, for example, Paul explains that the false believers in their congregation were brought in to spy on their freedom (Gal. 2:4). They did this, apparently, to "enslave" the congregation again.

Then, Paul argues eloquently that all the categories that divide people (including the categories of "free" and "slave") have disappeared in Jesus. Instead, he says, "you are all one" (Gal. 3:28). All this culminates in his great reminder, admonition, and promise: "It is for freedom Christ has set you free" (Gal. 5:1).

For Paul, freedom did not just mean "I am no longer a slave" or "I am not under the law." We were not set free from slavery or the law in order to live according to our own best guesses or desires, pleasing ourselves. Instead, this freedom is a whole way of being in the world, one to which

---

**Freedom is above all things the power to love. And it is not a power we could generate ourselves.**

---

Jesus called his people: a way of life. Being born from above frees us from the chains of sin, which function like addiction and prevent us from doing good. Freed from those chains, we are given the power to live the life that really is life: the life of mutual love and service. That power, that virtue, is called freedom. This is why Paul speaks to his flock in Galatia, reminding them what it is that they have been set free for: "For you were called to freedom, brothers and sisters; only do not use your freedom as an opportunity for self-indulgence, but through love become slaves to one another. For the whole law is summed up in a single commandment, 'You shall love your neighbor as yourself'" (Gal. 5:13–14).

What an amazing paradox. We are called to freedom, but through love we should be slaves to one another. We are not bound to the Jewish ceremonial law, but empowered to live out what it represents: the love of God expressed in our love of

our neighbors. The heart of God is to love. Keeping these two great commandments is freedom.

WHAT DOES JESUS HIMSELF SAY about freedom in the Gospels? Everything. The whole gospel of Jesus, the good news of the kingdom and the way he lived and worked, is a proclamation of freedom. Jesus is portrayed, among other things, as the new and greater Moses, leading his people out of slavery to freedom, delivering them into a land – his kingdom – marked by freedom. Luke's Gospel recounts the beginning of Jesus' ministry of freedom, and we hear the words of Isaiah's prophecy again: "He has sent me to proclaim release to the captives and recovery of sight to the blind, to let the oppressed go free, to proclaim the year of the Lord's favor" (Luke 4:18–19).

These verses, Jesus announces, have been fulfilled that day in the hearing of those listening. It is Jesus who frees the captives. He brings freedom. Freedom is a pillar of his ministry. But freedom is precisely the freedom of a new covenant, a new treaty of self-giving and mutual obligation. Jesus' promise is salvation and grace through his blood. To enter into this covenant, we repent. We believe the good news – that this is indeed the hour of God's offer of freedom, that Christ did not stay dead. And we are baptized, passing through those waters to freedom as the children of Israel passed through the Red Sea, in the baptism that is the sign of the new covenant as circumcision was of the old. Repent, believe, and be baptized. And then, live the life of freedom, the life in the kingdom. In other words, follow Jesus as your Master, as your King.

Jesus' ministry is one of healing and exorcism. He thinks of both of these as "setting free" those who are in bondage. In the story of the woman who had been crippled for eighteen years, Jesus' words of healing are (in part): "Woman, you are set free" (Luke 13:12). When he is challenged on this healing, he makes an argument about freedom – the sickness is bondage, and the healing is liberation: "You hypocrites! Does not each of you on the sabbath untie his ox or his donkey from the manger, and lead it away to give it water? And ought not this woman, a daughter of Abraham whom Satan bound for eighteen long years, be set free from this bondage on the sabbath day?" (Luke 13:15–16).

John tells how Jesus heals an invalid at the pool of Bethesda who had lain there for thirty-eight years in hope of healing. Jesus sees his plight and asks him a very important question: "Do you want to be healed?" (John 5:6). In some sense Jesus asks us the same question, in a different form: Do you want to be free?

What is this freedom? We return again to the idea of positive freedom, the freedom to be able to do good. In words at the center of John's Gospel, Christ speaks directly to the freedom he is offering:

> So Jesus said to the Jews who had believed him, "If you abide in my word, you are truly my disciples, and you will know the truth, and the truth will set you free." They answered him, "We are offspring of Abraham and have never been enslaved to anyone. How is it that you say, 'You will become free'?"
>
> Jesus answered them, "Truly, truly, I say to you, everyone who practices sin is a slave to sin. The slave does not remain in the house forever; the son remains forever. So if the Son sets you free, you will be free indeed." (John 8:31–36)

By its very nature, freedom evades capture by thought or word. Like the Holy Spirit, the Spirit of freedom, it cannot be pinned down. But we

know it. We feel it. Freedom is above all things the power to love. And it is not a power we could generate ourselves. We were enslaved, after all: to the devil, to the fear of death, to the weakness of our own flesh, our own sin. But "God so loved the world, that he gave his only Son, that whoever believes in him should not perish but have eternal life" (John 3:16). Only Jesus Christ can set us free. And if the Son sets you free, you will be free indeed. ➤

J. Kirk Richards, *Riding the Billows*, oil, 2024.

# The Autonomy Trap

## *A Conversion Story*

**JAMES R. WOOD**

REMEMBER THE MOMENT I told myself I would never talk to my dad again. I was sixteen years old, and my dad's adoptive parents had just surprised me with my first car: a bright yellow used Geo Tracker (that I would soon trade for a truck). After a slight disagreement, we split into separate vehicles to drive back to my mother's house. In the other car my dad was drinking while driving my little brother, and I drove my new car with his new wife. When we arrived at my mom's, she chastised my dad because we were much later than expected (at this time we did not have cell-phones) and she noticed the alcohol on his breath. He got out and yelled at her. And then he took my keys and told me he was going to tell my grand-parents I didn't want the car. For the first time in

All photography by Yalim Vural.

my life, I gave verbal expression to the anger I had internalized for years: "Get out of here. You can't treat us like this. We don't need you."

I come from a stock of relationship-quitters. During my childhood, pretty much everyone in my life had divorced at least once, extended family connections were strained, long-term friends were nonexistent, and moves were frequent. Over time I came to adopt a conception of freedom that had destroyed the lives of many around me, and which would threaten to destroy my own as well: the popular idea of freedom as unconstrained choice. Since this is impossible, the default was a more achievable version: the ability to drop commitments and relationships at any point when they become too complicated. Freedom as the license to leave when things get tough. Live by the mantra of Robert De Niro's character in *Heat*: "Don't let yourself get attached to anything you are not willing to walk out on in thirty seconds flat if you feel the heat around the corner." If complications come, don't worry. You can always go.

I eventually came to see that such freedom left me and some of those I loved unfree to love and to be known in love. Furthermore, this approach to freedom is a form of self-harm that also harms those dependent on you.

As Andrew Root has explained in his masterful work *The Children of Divorce*, divorce affects kids at a fundamental level. Their memories are tarnished and their family relations are frayed. Did we truly have any happy moments? Were we ever a loving family? Which cousins can we see now? Where will we go for holidays? How do we navigate the family gossip about our parents? Do we need to choose sides? Will we lose connection with those on one side of the family if we live with one parent as opposed to the other?

Children always complicate things – especially social theories that are fundamentally grounded in the autonomous individual. Children expose the lie that we are primarily individuals who only enter relationships voluntarily according to rational self-interest. The involuntary nature of

---

> I came to adopt a conception of freedom that had destroyed the lives of many around me, and which would threaten to destroy my own as well . . . freedom as the license to leave when things get tough.

---

the most important things in life can be experienced both for good or ill. No, we are not free to choose our parents, and that is a good thing: we do not choose to come into the world; our existence is the pure gift of our parents to us.

But the unchosen can be a curse as well. In divorce, children are not free to grow up in an intact family. And things are often (though not always) made worse with the introduction (and often quick exit) of new parent-alternatives. I had hoped that Michael, my mother's first husband after my dad, would take care of us, would show the warmth to my brother and me that my father never did, would be a safe person for my mom. I mean, he even played guitar. We would sing together. But the emotional outbursts began shortly and became recurrent. And then one day he was gone. By the time John entered the scene a couple of years later, I had already built up defenses, and I kept him at a distance, certain that things wouldn't work out and that he too would abandon us. Which is what happened. Frequent moves and multiple marriages meant that relationships were always on trial, always conditional. Best to hijack rejection by preemptively refusing to connect.

---

*James R. Wood is an assistant professor at Redeemer University in Ontario. He is the cohost of the Theopolis Institute's* Civitas Podcast *and a Commonwealth Fellow at the Davenant Institute.*

As C. S. Lewis vividly explained, connection makes you vulnerable: "To love at all is to be vulnerable. Love anything and your heart will be wrung and possibly broken." This is inevitable. For some, though, the lesson is rubbed in one's face early and often. Love, I learned, is not safe.

---

Safety, I assumed, required freedom from commitment, something as close to full autonomy as possible. But this freedom had left me enslaved to an untethered, empty self.

---

Commitment is not real. What is safe is hardened independence, especially toward these parental figures. And for me this began to trickle into other relationships.

We moved every year or so, and thus I was always the "new kid." This meant I had to regularly audition for friend groups. Since I wasn't particularly funny or cool, I tried to ingratiate myself with others by letting them copy my homework – because at least I was a decent student. Later I would make friends through basketball, which became my first love. When things got difficult in a friendship, as inevitably happens, I would quickly abandon the relationship, knowing we would likely move soon anyway.

In eighth grade, I was living with my best friend's family so I could finish the school year before rejoining my own family, who had moved to a new city. Right before one of our basketball games, I got in an argument with him and, instead of resolving it, I just phoned my mom to come get me and take me to our new home.

Commitment was for suckers, I was convinced. But what I eventually came to learn was that this "safety" was not so safe after all. Was I ever known? Did I even know myself? With whom was I connected in an enduring way? Was anything

stable? Would anyone stick with me? Am I simply unlovable? Are we all alone?

Lewis was correct – safety through hardening is no real safety at all:

> If you want to make sure of keeping [your heart] intact you must give it to no one, not even an animal. Wrap it carefully round with hobbies and little luxuries; avoid all entanglements. Lock it up safe in the casket or coffin of your selfishness. But in that casket, safe, dark, motionless, airless, it will change. It will not be broken; it will become unbreakable, impenetrable, irredeemable.

I gave more and more of myself to school and sports, all the while running from difficult relationships. I became increasingly anxious. On perpetual trial in friendships, and never reaching the other side of conflict, I became excessively defensive with others. Because I had no real experience of commitment, every relationship felt fragile, and thus every conflict existential.

During most of my childhood, we were poor and isolated. Moving all the time, having burned our bridges with the rest of the family, our little world consisted of our three-person unit: my mom, my brother, and myself. This led to a constant sense of crisis. When financial hardships would arise, it felt that we were a hair's breadth from homelessness. This is not an exaggeration. We spent years in group homes; then, for a brief time, we had no secure living situation at all. I came to believe deep down that there was no one who cared about our problems and that we were on our own. As the oldest son, this weighed particularly heavily on me, especially since my brother suffers from a fairly severe disability. Who would take care of everyone if not me?

This brings me back to my dad. He didn't really know how to fill the role of father. He never knew his own dad and was abandoned by his mother when he was very young. Throughout his life he struggled with substance abuse and anger, which didn't go away when, as a twenty-two-year-old high-school dropout, he was presented with a baby: me. Our relationship was always fraught and, at some point early on, I embraced the internal mantra: "I don't need you. You can't hurt me because I never needed you anyway." I would take care of myself and my family, so I assumed. If you want to be free of depending on others, you cannot be a burden on them. And thus, a subtle, secondary mantra also slipped in: "Don't be a burden." I never wanted to need anyone, and I assumed life was mine to figure out. As a kid with a somewhat responsible disposition, I did pretty well through elementary and high school. I could do the work and mostly get ahead. "Just don't mess up, and you will be fine." For years my father and I didn't talk.

Fast forward to college, when I had come to the end of my rope. I had gotten into a good school, but I was in over my head. And my relational deficiencies were getting impossible to ignore. By the end of my freshman year, I was struggling with a deep depression. I was surrounded by peers, especially as a member of a fraternity, and yet felt completely alone. And it wasn't necessarily others' fault. I didn't know how to connect; I got too upset in conflict; I kept running away from engaging. I would even notice myself at parties trying to quickly find a way out of conversations because I ran out of witty things to say and didn't want to burden others with my presence. In the film *High Fidelity*, John Cusack's character says, "I've committed to nothing . . . and that's just suicide . . . by tiny, tiny increments." Those tiny increments eventually gathered enough steam in my life to generate suicidal thoughts.

Those who don't come from a similar background probably struggle to understand what it is like to have no solid relational basis from which to approach the world. Folks who come from similar backgrounds to mine are relationally and psychologically deficient. We are not "well-adjusted." This can make us quick to be defensive. When you have so little to fall back on, when you feel like

you are floating alone in this world, rejection feels more existential. You often try to harden yourself out of self-protection, but you end up at the same time thin-skinned. Consequently, you can become more and more alone. This was the path I was on. And some of my family members have taken very similar paths, with different inflections. "You can't be weak; don't be a burden; you are on your own; leave me alone."

Again, I had extended this logic to everyone: "I don't need you"; and this logic to myself: "Don't be a burden." This was producing anxiety, loneliness, and ingratitude. I never wanted to ask for help, but I was also increasingly confused about relationships. I couldn't figure out why things continued to sour so often, why I couldn't connect

and keep friends, why I would get so defensive. I started to turn inward, but what I found there didn't provide answers or resolution. This is when the depression hit.

Safety, I assumed, required freedom from others: freedom from commitment, something as close to full material and psychological autonomy as possible. But freedom from others had left me enslaved to an untethered, empty self. In these times it became obvious that the freedom I was pursuing turned out to be utter isolation. Maybe I could just unburden the world of my presence.

And that's when I encountered God. A campus missionary named Ben had visited my fraternity, offering to meet with folks who wanted to talk about God, spiritual realities, etc. I gave him my contact information, and we met up a few times over coffee. What began to strike me was that he continued to reach out even though it was clear I could really offer him nothing. There was nothing he needed from me. He was just there and he cared. He asked about my life and tried to help me think about God. In one of my darkest hours that year, he asked me if I was happy with my life. It was a blunt, almost offensive question, but absolutely timely. I answered negatively, and he asked if I wanted that to change. He didn't sell me religion as a quick fix, or an intellectual affirmation. Instead, he invited me to join him on a summer trip with a group of Christian college students. I was at the end of my rope. I agreed.

That summer I found Christ, through the community of these friends. I observed how they loved each other (John 13:35). It was their hospitality to me that broke down all my defenses. I asked many of them, "Why are you like this?" And, with unique variations, they all answered by talking about Jesus. Above all, they seemed connected, they seemed rooted: they were people who had known the security of connection to Christ, and that secure standing opened up the possibility of real relationships with others. That summer I devoted my life to figuring out who this Christ was and what it meant to follow him.

What I received was myself. I was given myself. I was given true community, and a cause worth living for. I realized that I am not my own, but belong body and soul to my Savior, who gave himself for me. My fitting response of gratitude for that great, undeserved gift is to honor him with my life and serve others. And in this new life I found fellowship. I cannot tell you how much the church has meant to me. I know that there are people bound to me, and I to them. I am not alone. As Jesus promised, I have received *now* "houses and brothers and sisters and mothers" (Mark 10:30). I know that even though I bring burdens, as we all do, my brothers will help me "bear" them (Gal. 6:2). They are not mine alone to carry. I get to live. I get to be connected. I get to be grateful.

This is something I think my dad struggled to grasp. Shortly after my conversion, we were reconciled. It is one of the most profound gifts of my life that God provided me with that reconciliation. When I became a Christian, my heart softened toward my father. I began to consider the brokenness he had endured, and I longed to show him compassion as I had received undeserved compassion myself. So I began to reach out and attempt to connect. One night, months later, we had a deep heart-to-heart, and both

asked forgiveness. Then, a couple years later, he surprised my fiancée and me with a costly gift. He was a truck driver, and had saved up for months. He wanted to pay for our honeymoon. It was a symbol that he was trying now to be a dad. It was him moving toward connection, as his life had been even more isolating than my own.

Things continued to improve between us, and when I had my first two daughters, they loved playing with their "Pawpaw." The other two, and the one who is on the way, will never get to know him because as we were driving across the country so that I could start my PhD studies, I received the call that he had taken his own life. I still don't really understand it, and I haven't processed it completely. But I do know this: I am deeply grieved that he missed out on continuing to connect with and bless our kids, who loved him. I think he felt he was a burden on the rest of the family, and he couldn't see much hope for the remaining years of his life.

But he was not a burden on us; he was a gift. I wish he could have understood that. I wish he and others who struggle in loneliness and depression could know the freedom to love and be known in love.

That is the freedom for which Christ has set us free: the freedom to love. I found this in Christ and the community created by his cross (Eph. 2:11–22). What I needed was not freedom from others, retaining an easy opt-out clause for every relationship. What I needed was a relationship with the one who is "nearer to me than I am to myself," as Augustine said, and whose love frees me to know and be known by others, a freedom that leads to mutual service (Gal. 5). I needed freedom in fellowship, not freedom from commitment and obligation. I am so glad I have found it in the church. It's what I pray for others, what I desire for everyone whose grasped-for "freedom" has gone sour, whose lack of tether has led them to the end of themselves. You are not your own; you are not alone. ➤

# The Workers
## *and the* Church

*What happened to the Christian tradition of supporting the working class?*

**SOHRAB AHMARI**

"BEHOLD, THE WAGES of the laborers who mowed your fields, which you kept back by fraud, cry out" (James 5:4). This verse serves as the epigraph to my most recent book, *Tyranny, Inc.*, which documents the ways in which an asset-rich few lord it over the asset-less many, and explains why we need a renewal of the New Deal order that defined much of the American economic landscape in the middle twentieth century to overcome this state of affairs.

Given my reputation as a "public Catholic" of a theologically conservative bent, the book has caused not a little confusion on both ends of the political spectrum. In the *New York Times*, Michelle Goldberg has described me as "the right-winger calling for social democracy." Meanwhile, one of my many critics on the Reaganite right has labeled me a "pro-life New Dealer."

This crossing of ideological wires raises a vexing set of questions: Why is it that these days, it's considered unusual, even exotic, for small-o orthodox Christians to champion labor unions,

Petros Malayan, *Kond, Woman in Red*, 1989.

social democracy, and the legacy of Franklin Delano Roosevelt? Does traditional religion deserve its reputation as the upholder of existing material hierarchies, however unjust they may be? Why has that reputation come to attach itself to traditional religious communities? And how can we – I address myself to those who share my orthodoxy – shake off that reputation, as indeed we must?

*Behold, the wages you withheld cry out.* It's one of the most crystal-clear verses, among numerous others of the kind, both in the Hebrew Bible and the New Testament, that address the problem of just and unjust wages. Or to put it more sharply: verses that condemn unjust wages. The *Catechism of the Catholic Church* cites that verse from James, as well as Leviticus and Deuteronomy, in identifying unjust wages as one of the sins that cry out to heaven for divine vengeance. Yet today, the conservative corners of the Catholic Church in America are decidedly silent when it comes to widespread job and health precarity, systematically low wages, eye-watering inequality, the hollowing out of the real economy by Wall Street, and the destruction of the shared prosperity achieved by working people in the previous century. That is, when self-proclaimed "traditionalists" don't go out of their way to justify, in the name of orthodoxy, some of the worst abuses associated with today's model of neoliberal capitalism.

I T WASN'T ALWAYS THUS. In August 1889, dockworkers in London's East End mounted one of the longest and most consequential strikes in British labor history. The East London docks processed much of the trade that had catapulted Britain to global supremacy in the nineteenth century, generating the wealth that made possible the Victorian opulence satirized in the novels of Thackeray and Trollope, and whose aging relics to this day attract tourists. But for the workers who sought employment there, the docks were a site of hyperexploitation. I say "sought" because in addition to the permanent employees, some ten thousand itinerant workers, known as "casuals," would show up each day desperate for work and wages. But only about a third would be hired on any given day, and of these, few could obtain a full day's work and wages. This vast army of excess labor depressed wages for all dockworkers and made organizing them a steeply uphill battle.

Meanwhile, beyond the docks, the nearby slums inhabited by the dockers epitomized the working-class misery of the era. Here's how a French visitor described the scene:

> Street boys, bare-footed, dirty, and turning wheels to get alms. On the steps leading to the Thames they swarm. . . . More repulsive than the scum of Paris: without question, the climate is worse, and the gin more deadly. [As for the grownups,] it is impossible to imagine before seeing them how many layers of dirt an overcoat or a pair of trousers could hold; they dream or doze openmouthed. Their faces are begrimed, dull, and sometimes streaked with red lines. It is in these localities that families have been discovered with no other bed than a heap of soot; they have slept there during several months.

Compounding the physical deprivation was the routine social and psychological humiliation of the dockworkers. The socialist politician and labor leader Ben Tillett, himself a docker, noted how workers who couldn't find work would

> tramp hour after hour round the dock . . . picking the rubbish heaps . . . of refuse. . . . [This] was at times the only means of living and of hope

---

*Sohrab Ahmari is a founder and editor of* Compact, *and a contributing writer for the* New Statesman. *He has worked as the op-ed editor of the* New York Post *and as a columnist for the* Wall Street Journal. *He lives in New York.*

to many. No wonder the contractors called the casuals dock rats. The dock labourer came in for the foulest contempt. . . . All of us who were dock labourers concealed the nature of our occupation from our families as well as our friends.

It was against this bleak backdrop that on August 12, 1889, the dockworkers resolved to organize themselves at a mass gathering led by Tillett and two other activists. Their demands were modest and eminently reasonable: a pay raise, overtime wages, and the guarantee of at least four hours' work daily for each docker. The dock directors, however, refused to even consider the proposal, and so the Great London Dock Strike of 1889 erupted.

On August 16, when the owners continued to ignore the workers' demands, Tillett led a rally of some ten thousand dockers that garnered national and international news coverage for the strike.

Soon, a strike headquarters and fund were established, where sympathetic outsiders, especially clergy, delivered boxes of food. Activist women, including Karl Marx's daughter Eleanor, played an important role in supplying and organizing the headquarters and in the distribution of food rations to the striking workers and their families. Forced to publicly defend the abysmal wages they paid their workers, the owners were forthright: *if they paid a decent wage, it would cut into shareholder dividends, and that was intolerable.* This was long before large employers had the benefit of today's slick PR firms and the euphemistically named "union-avoidance" industry.

In response to this callousness, workers in many adjacent sectors mounted solidarity strikes, and soon the industrial action was threatening the stability of the whole British economy. Her Majesty's Government was forced to enlist soldiers

Petros Malayan, *Yerevan Metro Construction*, 1985.

as well as convict labor to unload strategic material from ships otherwise unable to deliver their wares. Still, the dock directors wouldn't budge, hoping instead that they could starve the dockers into submission as strike funds were depleted. Things, in short, were dire, both for workers and the political community as a whole.

Into this maelstrom entered an unlikely labor negotiator. In the early days of September 1889, Henry Edward Manning, the Catholic cardinal-archbishop of Westminster, left his palace to address both sides of what was fast becoming a scene of industrial war. To the workers, he urged calm and nonviolence. As one of the strike leaders recounted, this prince of the Church "spoke to the dockers in such a quiet, firm and advising,

fatherly manner that minute by minute, as he was speaking, one could feel the mental atmosphere changing." To the managers and dock owners, meanwhile, he preached their duties of social justice. Joined by the mayor of London, the acting commissioner of police, and sometimes the Anglican bishop of the city, Manning would press the bosses into granting the workers' demands.

Manning was born in Hertfordshire in 1808, the son of a prosperous banker. Tall and gaunt, he showed promise in athletics and considered the political life before becoming an Anglican parish priest. In 1851, he was received into the Catholic Church, right about the same time as that other great Victorian convert whom he would view as a rival for the rest of their lives: Saint John Henry

Petros Malayan, *Kond, Laundry*, 1989.

Newman. In 1865, Manning was made the archbishop of Westminster, and a decade later he was elevated to the cardinalate.

This was at a time when the longstanding legal handicaps against English Catholics were being gradually dismantled. Even so, a profound anti-Catholicism persisted at the cultural level. Upper-class converts like Newman and Manning, especially, were seen as adopting the superstition of Irish maids. Both men also came to defend the doctrine of papal infallibility issued by the First Vatican Council: Newman in more nuanced and literary fashion, Manning with simple, uncompromising devotion to the new dogma.

Alongside his theological orthodoxy and ecclesiastical conservatism, Manning displayed a constant concern for the fate of the poor and Britain's working-class masses – and a revulsion for the era's obscene class-based inequalities. "The homes of the poor in London are often very miserable," he observed in 1874, a decade before he was appointed to a royal commission on the working-class housing crisis. "These things cannot go on, these things ought not to go on. The accumulation of wealth in the land, the piling up of wealth like mountains in the possession of classes or individuals, cannot go on."

Manning found this combination of views – religious orthodoxy married to social justice – perfectly coherent. Indeed, his commitment to social justice and his opposition to class-based oppression flowed from his orthodoxy. And it was just this that led him to intervene in the dock strike. Initially, the employers refused his entreaties, but Manning's moral authority was decisive in leading other captains of industry to put pressure on the dock owners to make concessions and thus save the economy.

The dock directors indicated a willingness to make some concessions, but still not enough to end the strike. By early September, the mayor of London convened a conciliation committee composed of six members, including Cardinal Manning, who soon came to play the leading role. He spoke for the workers and demanded decency from the employers; he cajoled the strike committee into accepting compromises, though the final peace would require still greater exertions from the aging cardinal.

S O WHAT HAPPENED? Why is it that Cardinal Manning's agenda strikes us as an oddity? Why is it that many Americans today associate traditional faith or religious orthodoxy with a dogmatic devotion to tax cuts for the wealthy and hostility to organized labor and social welfare? Why is it that the Reaganite gospel has come to occlude, well, the genuine article?

Here, I can only write from within my own Roman Catholic tradition, though I suspect my claims will resonate, at least in their broad outlines, with many of those belonging to other denominations and faith groups.

In our time, too many Christians have come to serve as apologists for "things that cannot go on," owing to three broad trends. Each of these deplorable turns correlates theological developments with certain material conditions, in the life of the church and that of wider society. To be sure, ideas, including theological ones, have their own inner integrity, and they aren't strictly reducible to class-based or economic formations, as a certain kind of vulgar Marxism would have it. But is it not also possible to reform religious ideas without addressing the material substrate on which they rest. Historic Christianity, especially, has never operated that way – on a purely immaterial plane. Christians are called to pay due respect to the mundane aspect of what it means to be human: its ordinary joys and miseries, and the ways in which the social backdrop of our lives can open us to divine love and the love of neighbor – or shut us out. After all, we profess that God himself came to inhabit those ordinary joys and miseries.

The first deplorable turn, then, is precisely the denial that human beings are social and political animals. Our sociality is a premise not of supernatural revelation, but of natural reason: more specifically, classical political philosophy. If human beings are indeed naturally social and political, as the Greco-Roman tradition insisted, then our religious lives are inextricably bound up with our social lives. Or to put it in explicitly Christian terms, individual salvation is bound up with, and dependent on, social salvation. Religious believers who hold otherwise must end up reaffirming a rupture between philosophy and theology, or reason and revelation, that forces them to choose between unreasonable faith

just to make ends meet, she won't have the time or the energy or even the sense of predictable regularity in her schedule necessary to play and do homework with her kids, let alone transmit her faith; the children will very likely be babysat by screens. And those screens, incidentally, are under the control of Silicon Valley oligarchs who have every incentive to addict children via algorithmic manipulation, even if it means the proliferation of suicide content, content promoting eating disorders, and hardcore pornography.

How we organize our society and economy structures the belief and the "moral conditions"

---

Civility and virtue are central to the good life, but it is a betrayal of two-and-a-half millennia of virtue ethics to pretend that we can develop a virtuous citizenry while maintaining a ruthlessly competitive political economy.

---

(superstition, fundamentalism) and a soulless, pinched account of reason (scientism, relativism).

We should reject this unhealthy dichotomy. We should resist the rupture between reason and revelation. And if we do, it follows that human beings' *natural* status – as social animals – doesn't go away in their dealings with the things of God. We are still social animals when we kneel at the foot of our bed to pray (or lay down a prayer mat facing Mecca in a corner of our study). And the way we organize our society contours the spiritual lives of its members. Social organization, the way we structure our economy, regulates the conditions of access not just to material goods but to spiritual ones as well.

This is by no means to imply that the poor lack access to faith. Very often, it is they who, like the widow in the gospel, give their last cent to the Lord (Mark 12:41–44). The outrage is that our economic system would deprive them of even that last cent. If a single mother has to work two precarious, gigified jobs in the new economy

of ordinary people, as Cardinal Manning might have said. This was obvious to historic Christianity, because it was obvious to the classical philosophy that the church made her own and purified beginning in late antiquity. Yet today it is a kind of lost wisdom, and self-proclaimed "conservative" or "traditionalist" Christians are often the most likely to be repelled by it.

Earlier this year, for example, when Jordan Peterson harangued Pope Francis for supposedly "saving the planet" instead of "saving souls," the Canadian psychologist and pundit found his most receptive audience among the "trads" and conservative Christians. Right-wing Catholic influencers and media outlets rewarded him with reposts and praise, not pausing for a second to consider the public claims of their own church, let alone the demands of filial piety. Think of it as American Catholicism's version of trading a birthright for a mess of pottage.

The birthright in question is a church that rejects the dis-integration of life's various realms and insists, instead, on their proper ordering in relation to each other. The Catholic tradition teaches that you can't neatly partition politics from metaphysics, the economy from morality, culture from spirituality, and salvation from how we treat the planet, "our common home" (as the subtitle of Francis's 2015 encyclical on ecology, *Laudato si'*, has it). Starting from these premises, the Church has intervened in the crises of modern life long before Francis assumed the Petrine office.

In 1891, Pope Leo XIII published *Rerum novarum,* his encyclical on capital and labor that rejected socialism, even as it called on public authorities – note well: not merely the charity of employers – to ensure a living wage and the right of workers to organize in defense of their mutual interests. In 1937, amid the rise of Nazi racism and anti-Semitism, Pope Pius XI denounced these tendencies in *Mit brennender Sorge* (notably offering it in German, rather than the typical Latin). And in 1963, as the Cold War logic of nuclear brinksmanship and mutually assured destruction took hold and plunged the whole species into anxiety, Pope John XXIII called for disarmament in *Pacem in terris.*

One could cite many other examples; these are just three of the most prominent historical interventions. The point is that the popes have never confined themselves strictly to "religious stuff," as Peterson types would have it. For one thing, their teaching authority extends to "faith and morals," and that second part covers a lot of ground. Morals, for example, implicate justice: what is owed to each person and to the human species at large and the planet entrusted to our stewardship. As such, the "religious stuff" Peterson wants Pope Francis to focus on necessarily implicates law, economics, politics, and ecology. These and other material conditions structure the church's relations with the world. A church that ignored them – or a religious community, to frame it more broadly, that didn't pay heed to the conditions of access to faith – couldn't fulfill its mission.

And yet there exists a vast apparatus of "conservative" think tanks, journals, publishing houses, and online influencers whose central purpose is to convince traditional believers otherwise: that the crises they deplore in the "culture" (alienation, atomization, low rates of family formation and fertility, and so on) have nothing whatsoever to do with the neoliberal economic model and the obscene inequalities in power and wealth it generates.

Assuaging the consciences of the donor class, while helping to uphold its economic power, these ideological institutions demand that we believe the incredible: that the miseries and dysfunctions of downscale America – the spiraling deaths of despair, declining life expectancy, the fact that "working class" has become synonymous with out-of-wedlock births and opioid addiction – all these and more are simply a matter of individual failure. Millions and millions of individual failures of virtue that we can only hope might be corrected by heroic individual effort on the part of the poor, with assistance from conservative think tankers and authors writing books and articles with titles like *The Soul of Civility* and "Stuck with Freedom, Stuck with Virtue." Civility and virtue *are* central to the good life, to be clear, but it is a gross betrayal of two-and-a-half millennia of virtue ethics to pretend that we can develop a virtuous citizenry while maintaining a ruthlessly competitive political economy divested of all virtue.

THE SECOND DEPLORABLE PHENOMENON is related to the first: self-help ideology, which has returned with a vengeance. In truth, the brand of "traditionalism" we have been discussing has roots that can be traced not to the gospel or the magisterium of the Catholic Church, but to the Whiggish self-help ideology that emerged in the mid-nineteenth century as a means to tame the democratic, populist backlash engendered by America's nascent market society.

Back then, an emerging professional class reframed the stresses and miseries that bore down on the poor as defects of individual character. Benjamin Rush, the Founding Father and Philadelphia physician, averred that "disease is a habit of wrong action, and all habits of injurious tendency are diseases." To steel themselves against the yearning for leisure, Americans had to adopt teetotalism, sparse herbal diets, and cold showers. Young men joined clubs featuring military-style discipline: early curfews, exercise in the dawn hours. Evangelical Protestantism, which had once sanctified the anti-market (and anti-slavery) ethos of backcountry democrats, came to narrowly promote individual salvation. Ralph Waldo Emerson preached that the harsh "laws of property" would be transfigured into "universality," if only young men of means would "let into it the new and renewing principle of love."

While he campaigned against slavery, William Lloyd Garrison urged Northern workers against making trouble for bosses, counseling them toward individual self-betterment. The abolitionist brothers Arthur and Lewis Tappan founded the country's first credit-rating agency, which specially flagged men with "intemperate habits," those drawn to the "sporting life," and those leading "large and expensive families" – that last measure of creditworthiness, as the historian Charles Sellers argues, was one of several disciplinary mechanisms that helped slash birth rates to 2.8 children per married woman by the latter years of the nineteenth century, down from 6.4 in 1800. The market squeezed American fecundity long before *Griswold v. Connecticut* and *Roe v. Wade*.

Admittedly, the substance of self-help in the mid-nineteenth century was quite different from its contemporary iterations. Yet its ultimate message echoes unmistakably today: social problems must be overcome by individual effort, even in the heart. Everywhere you look on Christian social media, you will find an excitable young man or woman staring into a phone camera and urging you to save your family from the Gehenna of modern life, mainly by making the right consumer choices: you have to homeschool; eat the right kind of primitive, organic wheat; escape chaotic urban cores and settle new frontiers; lift weights; earn enough so your wife can exit the formal labor force and assume her God-ordained submissive role; invest in crypto!

Traditional and conservative religious communities are drowning in privatism and "lifestyleism": the dream of a retreat to some boutique redoubt, away from the contaminated world. Some of these lifestyle recommendations are no doubt beneficial. There is nothing wrong with and probably much good about weightlifting or wholesome organic food or "classical education." But these things do not a Christian politics make. Moreover, the movement as a whole can only deepen the isolation and solipsism typical of the very modernity its advocates deplore, and it represents a profound betrayal of faith's public, social component – and especially of Christianity's character as a mass religion. A religion whose founder delighted in the company of children; who made a point of not letting the multitudes go home hungry; who launched his public ministry at a wedding, conjuring *wine*, that primordial aid to human conviviality and sociality; who proclaimed that "the Spirit of the Lord is upon me, because he has anointed me to preach good news to the poor" (Luke 4:18).

As the French patrologist and Vatican II expert Jean Daniélou emphasizes, "the poor" in Jesus' discourse aren't just the abjectly poor, though they're certainly included, but also the average masses: people who can't afford to retreat to boutique religious communities, who have to make do with public schools and ordinary parishes and so on. Jesus addressed himself to such people, even as he also gathered an elite to himself (not that the elite exactly measured up to the Master's demands when it really mattered at Gethsemane and Golgotha!). At Cana, when he wined and dined

the multitudes, Daniélou contends, Jesus expressed this "simple sense of community."

This is why Pope Francis speaks frequently of "a Church of the poor" or of "a poor Church for the poor." But I'm afraid that in certain quarters of American Christianity, the gated-community church or the elite-trad-lifestyle church is edging out the church of the poor. If you have ample time and economic freedom, you can develop your boutique spiritual life. You can even enjoy the ministry of priests (or pastors) who essentially serve as private chaplains to the affluent. But you don't care if your brothers and sisters lack the conditions of access to this spiritual life. And you might be blinkered by pride to your own deprivation as a result. Having abandoned the church of the poor – the church that places itself at the center of urban chaos, in the poverty shacks and messy conditions of the periphery – you never encounter the God-Man who appears as the least of his brethren: the homeless man or single mother or oppressed wage worker whose hands bear unmistakable stigmata visible to eyes of faith alone.

KNOWING MY CRITICS, I can already hear them grumbling that all my talk of neoliberalism and class conflict and rich and poor puts me in league with Marxists and socialists, those who view modern society as a scene of social conflict, rather than a space for freedom congenial to the Christian message. Which brings us to the third and final development: "conservative" believers' naturalization of social relations that are, in fact, perfectly contingent and thus should be subject to ruthless critique in the light of eternal truth.

Petros Malayan, *End of the Shift*, 1986.

Permit me to illustrate this with an example. One of my critics, a Catholic ethicist at a prominent business school, not too long ago published an essay in which he said, in effect: *Doesn't Ahmari know that with all this talk of unmasking hidden coercion and conflict in market society he is reenacting the discourse of leftists and feminists who seek to tear down everything that is orderly and established by pointing out the power dynamics lurking behind it all?*

It's a good question. My response in Catholic settings has typically been to read off any number of quotations from the popes in which they decry unrestrained capitalism and call for limits on accumulation. But initially, I tell my hearers that the quotation I'm about to read off comes from Karl

This Christian tradition of critical political economy raises a pair of related difficulties for the "traditionalist" Christian defenders of our present market arrangements. For one thing, they must at least implicitly concede – the more honest among them admit it openly – that they view Christian social teaching through ideological bifocals: the church's moral rejection of abortion, euthanasia, and similar practices is (correctly) treated as a moral absolute; by contrast, when the church cries out against the injustices of the market order and supports a living wage, labor unions, denser social safety nets, and the like, there is a relativization and a great deal of hemming and hawing – those are "prudential" matters, and anyway, the popes aren't trained economists, and

---

## Unlike secular Marxists, who dream of the abolition of one class by another, Christians are called to promote reconciliation between them.

---

Marx or Rosa Luxemburg or some other canonical leftist figure. Only afterward do I reveal that it was, say, Leo XIII in *Rerum novarum* who lamented "the enormous fortunes of some few individuals and the utter poverty of the masses" under industrial capitalism; or that it was Saint John Paul II in *Laborem exercens* who warned against "the *danger* of treating work as a special kind of 'merchandise,' or as an impersonal 'force' needed for production" and recalled "*the principle of the priority of labor over capital*" (emphases in original).

The strategy never fails to elicit a kind of uncomfortable laughter, even shock. But it's more than just an effective rhetorical trick: to read the social encyclicals is to be reminded that Christianity bears its own imperative for questioning existing material hierarchies. Marx and his progeny don't have a monopoly on the critique of exploitation inherent to, and the lopsided power dynamics generated by, a society based on commodity production.

so on. But that maneuver entails a relativization of the entire edifice of Christian justice, because the same fundamental premises undergird both the moral teachings that are taken as absolute and the economic teachings that are relegated to second-class status.

The second difficulty is more bedeviling still and more interesting for our purposes. It has to do with the fact that "trad" or "conservative" apologists for the status quo are (at least very commonly in the United States) objectively on the side of the most ferociously unconservative and socially and culturally destabilizing force in human history: capitalism. It's capitalism that reduces every human relationship to exchange value, constantly conjuring new desires in order to sustain demand for commodities, profaning all that is sacred, melting all that is solid into air.

This historical reality forces "conservative" and Christian apologists for the market order to focus relentlessly on various cultural evils, while pretending that "the culture" has no significant connection to economic organization. They might urge their readers to adopt "6 Ways to Detox from Marxist Feminism for a Happier Life," but they won't and can't account for the fact that if women are prioritizing their careers and education, it's partly in response to the "dull compulsion" of powerful economic imperatives.

That is to say, the corporate #GirlBoss feminism the trads rage against merely gives a lean-in gloss to what women are already compelled to do by the market: by a society in which the income needed to live comfortably alone, taking the national median, is just under $90,000 in 2024, while wages for the bottom half of earners have been stagnant for the better part of two generations, and the median single full-time worker earns about $60,000.

Nothing in traditional religion, rightly understood, obliges us to defend this state of affairs or to redirect popular discontent into self-help and mindless culture warring. More than that, traditional religion compels us to see – yes, after Marx – how a society centered around commodity production is constantly at risk of privileging the inanimate over the living, of subsuming social relations between living, breathing human beings into relations between things. Of all people, religious believers and Christians especially must reassert the primacy of people over things, labor over capital, subjects over objects.

B UT UNLIKE SECULAR MARXISTS, who dream of the abolition of one class of the living by another, Christians are called to promote reconciliation between them. What might that look like? As Cardinal Manning recognized in the course of the Great Dock Strike, true reconciliation involves counterpower mounted from below as much as exhortations to virtue from above. At its best, class reconciliation

invites spiritual realities that no material doctrine can account for.

At one point, as the ordeal of the strike entered its final stages and an agreement was close to hand, the full strike committee met the cardinal at a Catholic school in the East London district of Poplar. The cardinal addressed himself to uncompromising workers. Two of the labor leaders later recounted, "Just above [the cardinal's] head was a carved figure of the Madonna and Child, and some among the men tell how a sudden light seemed to swim around it as the speaker pleaded for the wives and children. When he sat down, all in the room knew in their own minds that [Manning] had won the day."

Finally, on September 14, a formal bargain was struck that soon came to be known as the "Cardinal's Peace." As a 2015 pamphlet by Britain's Unite union notes, "The following day, a final triumphant procession marched to Hyde Park." The procession included "a multitude of crosses placed in honour of Cardinal Manning." And when Henry Edward Cardinal Manning died in 1892, the London Trades Council passed a resolution that declared, "English, Irish, and Italian workers in London felt that by the death of Cardinal Manning, they had lost their very best friend."

"Behold, the wages of the laborers who mowed your fields, which you kept back by fraud, cry out." Perhaps what's needed is a wider apprehension of the insidious nature of sin, how it embeds itself not just in individual souls but in social and economic structures. Acknowledging this reality isn't tantamount to obviating individual responsibility. "The structure made me do it" isn't an apologia I'm going to try when I meet Saint Peter at the pearly gates. But it does imply a duty to be vigilant against structures that lead little ones astray, just as, at the individual level, we are called to avoid occasions of sin. Woe to those who acquiesce to an entire economy that is a vast and hideous occasion of sin. ↘

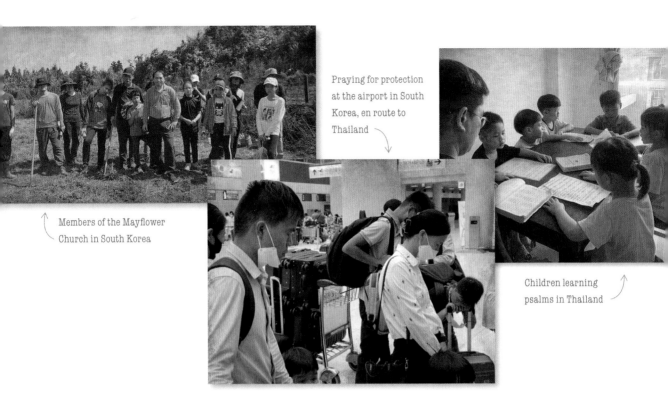

Members of the Mayflower Church in South Korea

Praying for protection at the airport in South Korea, en route to Thailand

Children learning psalms in Thailand

# An Exodus from China

*A persecuted house church chooses to flee together as a community.*

**PAN YONGGUANG**

*Sixty-three members of the Mayflower Church finally landed in Texas on Good Friday 2023, three years after the group fled China and sought asylum. Plough's Sam Hine interviews their pastor, Pan Yongguang, about their sojourn.*

**Plough: Let's start at the beginning. How did you become a Christian in China?**

**Pan Yongguang:** On the day my father died in a car accident, some Christians came to the hospital and preached the gospel to me. After that, I went to church with them. I attended the church's Bible study for two years, constantly asking questions and debating, but never praying. Then I read Jesus' words: "Healthy people do not need a doctor, but sick people do. I came not to call the righteous, but sinners." That night I admitted that I was a sinner and prayed to God. I was baptized at Easter in 2003.

**Why did you end up leading an illegal house church?**

The person who preached the gospel to me was a member of a house church. As my faith matured, I realized that the Three-Self Church authorized by the atheist Communist Party of China is not true Christianity but a tool for ideological rule. In China, the house churches are the true churches that follow the teachings of the Bible. When I became a pastor, I knew that if I established a house church it would inevitably be suppressed by the government, and I was ready and willing to pay the price.

**Can you give an example of harassment you and your church faced in China?**

The church in China has been repressed since the Communist Party came to power in 1949. Ideological control relaxed as part of China's admission into the World Trade Organization in 2001, but repression has intensified significantly since Xi Jinping came to power in 2013. My city, Shenzhen, is adjacent to Hong Kong and is known as the most open and dynamic city in China, but the church there has also faced severe repression. For many years, the secret police monitored my movements and often asked me to report on church activities. Many times during worship, the police barged in and forced us to stop.

**Paul writes, "It is for freedom that Christ has set us free" (Gal. 5:1). What did that verse mean to you while living under state repression?**

Christ has set us free and made us free. We are not bound by sin, so we have more strength to endure and persevere in our faith in the face of repression. Just like it was for Christian slaves in the Roman Empire or black slaves before the American Civil War, this spiritual freedom is precious, but it is far better to be truly free from state repression as well.

**Why did you decide it was time to leave China?**

Faced with increasing pressure from the government, we had wanted to leave for a few years, to escape. We imagined that when Xi Jinping stepped down, we would come back. We never thought about never coming back, let alone everyone going to the United States. In late 2019 and early 2020 we went in smaller groups to Jeju Island, South Korea, a holiday destination for Chinese people, and then applied for asylum there.

**Did any members choose to stay behind?**

We fully respect the free choice of each member, and about one-third remain in China. The situation of each family is different, and there are many reasons for choosing to stay in China. The members who remain in China are currently facing even more severe persecution because we left. We still keep in touch, but for security reasons we don't contact them often.

**It took over three years before you finally found refuge in the United States. Looking back, what were some of the most memorable moments on your journey?**

After a long period of no work, in the winter of 2020 a Korean pastor found us an hourly job pulling radishes in the fields. As professionals, none of us had done fieldwork or any tiring physical labor before. On the first morning, I was worried about sending my thirteen-year-old son to the fields at 5 a.m. He said to me, "Dad, don't worry. Look, I'm as tall as you." He came back in the evening, very tired and happy. Not only did he get his wages, he also brought back two radishes. Two sisters, tired out from the work and missing their lives in China, sang Psalm 137: "By the rivers of Babylon we sat down, and we cried when we remembered Zion!"

In the spring of 2021, the cherry trees were blooming on Jeju Island. A young girl from the church happily ran up to me and asked, "Pastor, do you think my clothes are beautiful? I picked them up from the trash can yesterday." Looking at her smiling face, I couldn't help but turn away and cry.

**What were the most difficult moments?**

The most difficult moment was when we decided to move from South Korea to Thailand. Everything was uncertain and the future was unknown. That's when we all signed a "New Mayflower Compact" patterned on the one the Pilgrims made on the Mayflower before they arrived in the New World. Ours concludes like this: "We solemnly swear before God to unite, support, and never abandon one another, forming this sacred community. To further the objectives of this covenant, we pledge to fully adhere to and obey the Word of God. Relying on God's grace, we humbly seek his blessings."

In the winter of 2022, we were still stuck in Thailand. The weather was very warm, but my heart was cold. It was much more dangerous than in South Korea; there were Communist spies tracking and threatening us. For everyone's safety, our US supporters advised me to hide separately with my family and not contact the congregation. One evening, my wife and I took a walk and didn't return at the agreed time. My son and daughter cried and prayed; they thought their parents had been arrested.

**Eventually, though, you were all detained. Then, at the last minute, you were granted asylum in the United States, thanks to the political action of American Christians. What was that day like for you?**

I couldn't believe it was true. We fully expected that the Thai authorities would deport us back to China, as they had many others. The women and children, who had been separated from us, thought it was another deception and didn't dare to walk out of the prison until they saw the men outside the gate. An American consul came to pick us up. He told us in person: "Now I will take you to the airport to fly to the United States. The tickets have been purchased." We hugged and cried at the prison gate. I led everyone in singing a song, Psalm 126. We choked up while singing, the

prison guards were crying and recording videos with their mobile phones, and the American consul was crying and making the sign of the cross. Then the consul issued us visas. As I held mine, I thought of the movie *Schindler's List* and thanked the US government for including everyone in the Mayflower Church on its list. Boarding the plane to the United States, I still couldn't believe that what had happened was real.

**Your group is exceptional in that you fled together as a community. Did that make it harder or easier?**

Fleeing together as a community made things easier, because people who love and trust each other can help and care for each other. During the escape, we never felt abandoned, and we always encouraged each other.

But it also made things more difficult, especially because more than half of us were minors. It was difficult for us to hide, and we easily became the target of Communist Party surveillance. In terms of economic resources, we had to rely on support from others. Eight children were born during the escape, bringing our number to sixty-three, and it was particularly difficult to take care of newborns without medical insurance.

**Did the biblical story of Exodus resonate with you during your sojourn?**

I preached on Exodus for a year and a half before we left China, and the children watched *The Prince of Egypt* several times. The most important thing to me in these stories is that God's call is the decisive factor.

I know our long journey has been called a modern Exodus. It is a miracle that we could all enter the United States after several years. In the process, each person's courage and confidence in God proved indispensable. After we arrived in the United States, someone suggested my English name should be Moses. For me, that's complicated. I am deeply proud of it, but I know I often

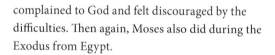
Detained members of the Mayflower church in a cell in Thailand

complained to God and felt discouraged by the difficulties. Then again, Moses also did during the Exodus from Egypt.

**What does community mean to you, after all you have been through together? Will you stick together now that you live in a highly individualistic society?**

I have known these families for more than ten years, some more than twenty years. I have watched every child grow up, and I am now the principal of the school and teach the children almost every day. We have a deep understanding, trust, and love for each other, and it is painful to be separated from each other.

I've told the congregation, "I am your pastor, not someone else's pastor; without you, I have no value." Members of the congregation have also told me, "Where the church is, my home is there." We are a very close community, and no one wants to separate. Coming to the highly individualistic society of the United States, we are sure to face temptations, but we are still very united now. The Pilgrims who came on the Mayflower four hundred years ago lived in a community for twenty-four years before they separated. I am not

sure how long we can stay together, but this is the direction I am working toward, because Jesus wants his saints to be gathered together.

**What challenges or obstacles does your group still face?**

How to preach the gospel and bear witness to the Lord Jesus in a completely new environment is our biggest challenge, and not knowing English is our biggest obstacle.

**How might fellow Christians support your new beginning?**

We have a vision to build a "Mayflower Community" here in Midland, Texas, where we have settled, with a Christian school in the community to teach children the Bible and Chinese and English. This community will become a refuge city for other Chinese people who are persecuted for their faith. All this is just in conception and will require the support of fellow Christians praying for us, visiting and encouraging us, and contributing to building our community. ➤

For more information on the Mayflower Church, visit *chinaaid.org/mayflower*.

Interview responses have been translated from Chinese.

# The Body She Had

*If only parents could be spared the terrible freedom
of being forced to choose.*

**ROSEMARIE GARLAND-THOMSON**

"MY HUSBAND AND I decided that it was a loving decision not to bring her into the world with the body that she had." This line from a recent newspaper article on abortion rights stays with me when I'm quiet in the early morning before my day of obligations and pleasures begins. This girl who is not in the world because of "the body that she had" had a body like mine and a body like those of many of my friends.

She was a girl with a body we now talk about as having a significant congenital disability. The piece referred to her as a "pregnancy," rather than the girl whose memory haunts me. Parents like hers, writes the journalist, "speak of the pregnancies they lost as unborn children." Her parents carried out what they believed to be their obligation to her by saving her from what they imagined was a life diminished by suffering and debility, a life not worth living.

Tim Lowly, *Parel*, acrylic on panel, 2014.

Over the decades of my long life, I have collected a strong and secure group of friends, mostly women. We are educators and writers, and we have bodies also understood as having significant congenital disabilities. Several of us are blind or partially blind; a few use wheelchairs; some are Deaf; there's some neurodiversity and a good amount of physical asymmetry. We all managed to get a good enough education to develop our capacities to talk, think, and write, often in unusual and unexpected ways. Most of our schools tolerated more than welcomed us, but felicitous temperaments and at least good-enough mothering gave us the building blocks of the good lives we all now inhabit. Like most everyone else with a life of flourishing and joy, we have lives shaped by a balance of good fortune and grit.

The difference between this girl who is not in the world and my friends and me who are in the world is that before we were born into the world, our parents did not know what kind of bodies we would have. We were born, for the most part, before the profiles, information, and images of the prenatal testing era sketched out our being and future for waiting parents. Now the bodies we have are named as medical conditions: syndromes, rare diseases, skeletal dysplasias, genetic anomalies, and more pathologies. These descriptions of our bodies pin us to the world like specimens in museums. Yet in truth we are the flesh and bone and blood that have lived our lives, done our work, thought our thoughts. With these bodies, we have loved and been loved by many others along our way.

When we appeared in the world, our parents were unsettled, even shocked. We simply showed up without a story. They had to take us in, and they did, even though certain aspects were unexpected and unwanted. They did not choose us: they held us in their arms because they had to. Some of us were indeed given away or locked away, but most of our parents held on to us despite their bewilderment. We were gifts that stretched our families' humanity, but no one much recognized that at the start. We made lives for ourselves from our circumstances and our temperaments, as do all our fellow humans, living as freely as

---

## We were gifts that stretched our families' humanity, but no one much recognized that at the start.

---

we could within the constraints of our place and time, our embeddedness in the world.

This girl with a body like ours who is not in the world might have had a life like ours. Her parents must not have known that when they made the "loving decision not to bring her into the world with the body that she had." I am unsettled by their decision, wanting them to know us, wanting to say to them that she would have been all right. Experiences much like the human variations and frailties we think of as disabilities come to all of us eventually. The girl who is not in the world and her parents might have learned this if she had joined us in this world.

The parents of that girl with a body like ours bear a terrible freedom. This freedom that modern liberal societies offer has often become a heavy mantle thrown over the shoulders of parents as they exercise their right – this onerous obligation – to choose who they bring into the world. The authority of a medical diagnosis and the life it predicts can overwhelm other possible stories of shared lives well lived.

While the intention of medicine and health care is making people as normal and healthy as possible, the outcomes of medical practice

---

*Rosemarie Garland-Thomson is professor emerita of English and bioethics at Emory University. She co-edited* About Us: Essays from the Disability Series of the New York Times.

often eliminate people disqualified from those categories. The parents of our lost girl had to imagine her and the woman she would become; they had to judge her future life before they had the chance to meet her. The choice they had is perhaps the most significant moral choice freedom presents because it determines who can and cannot enter our human community. This imagining, judging, and choosing are obligations that medicine has put before parents but for which they have almost no meaningful guidance.

This freedom to choose who enters the family and our shared community is constricted by the limited stories available to parents about possibilities for human flourishing. Most people do not know the stories of livable lives for girls who come into the world with bodies like mine and my friends'. Abandoned in the reproductive clinic, the parents of these lost children lack these stories. They must choose whether to "terminate the pregnancy," a moral action expressed in language that distances them from their daughter, already inhabiting her own tiny, hidden body, intent on coming into the world to join their family.

The parents of the girl with a body like ours who is not in the world were perhaps not offered much information beyond the medical context of their daughter's predicted health condition. They may not have known about the duties of government and community to care for and sustain their daughter and their family. The rigorous commitment to the freedom of self-determination and individual autonomy, as philosophers such as Alasdair MacIntyre point out, perhaps eclipsed a more communitarian moral obligation to welcome, embrace, and care for one another.

Decisions about what kinds of people to bring into our families and the world grow heavier as the array of reproductive medical technologies expands. We find ourselves with new options available: Should I have this screening? Should I use in vitro fertilization? How should I select embryos? What am I to make of a polygenic risk score? Utilitarian philosopher Peter Singer calls this "shopping at the genetic supermarket." All these freedoms, all these choices, and all this information is somehow in the interest of keeping people with bodies like mine and my friends' and the girl who is not in the world from joining our families and communities.

Until recently, parents could only begin intentionally shaping the being and lives of their children after they held their newborn child in their arms. The new human being, separated now from the body of her mother, insisted with her visible presence that she be recognized as a distinct person with a recognizable will of her own and a full moral and legal status. For the most part, laws, professional protocols, standards of practice, and communal traditions initiated at birth guide parents' choices and consent. Unsettled as any parent might be by a baby who is not what they expected, that baby enters into the world surrounded and supported by an array of people – lactation consultants, nurses, obstetricians, midwives, neonatologists, pediatricians, surgeons, grandparents, relatives, clergy, family friends – all of whom welcome the newborn to her community. People come bearing gifts: pink-and-blue hats, onesies, blankets; if necessary, intubation, medication, incubators, medical skill, spiritual guidance, and moral sweat. Her status as a newborn human protects this most vulnerable of beings. Parents stunned by the revelation of a baby who is different from what they expected or wanted are nonetheless invited to make the best of what they got.

This girl, placed in her mother's arms, squirming and squalling and demanding attention and care, has little relationship to the risk profiles, diagnoses, prognoses, prenatal testing, or leaflets that shape her parents' decision-making. These obscure the enfleshed person who is their daughter, hidden from them deeply in the womb. With only this pathological picture, her parents do not yet know her in the human ways that we know and recognize one another. An increasingly

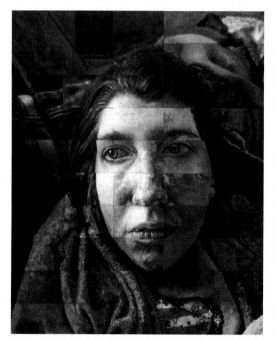

Tim Lowly, *At 25* (front and reverse), acrylic, gold leaf, foil, gold pigment, and glitter on wood, 2010

**About the artist:** Tim Lowly is a Chicago-based artist, curator, musician, and teacher. His daughter, Temma, who has cerebral palsy with spastic quadriplegia, is a central subject of his work. Below, he explains the paintings accompanying this article.

*Parel* (page 64): "In Vermeer's iconic painting *Meisje met de parel* (Girl with a Pearl Earring) the pearl could be understood as suggesting the young woman possesses a beauty as 'pure' as a pearl. That said, it seems possible that in the context of seventeenth-century Netherlands, the painting might have been perceived as being about desirability. This understanding of the painting might be corroborated by the girl's gaze. By contrast, in this painting, Temma does not engage the viewer. At one point when my wife Sherrie was looking at the painting she said, 'It looks like a pearl.' She might have been referring to the surface of the paint, but I think there's a way that the painting points to the mysterious translucence and opacity of Temma's presence as something like – and, curiously, as beautiful as – a pearl."

*"At 25* [above] was made as a kind of commemoration of twenty-five years of working with my daughter Temma as a subject and a collaborator in my art. The piece is composed of twenty-five sections, each of which is painted by one or two artists from around the world. For the front of the image I provided the participants with a section of a portrait photograph corresponding to the piece they were given. I also gave them black and white matte acrylic (the paint I usually use) and asked them to render the photograph as stylistically neutrally as possible. For an artist to set aside their style is a significant gesture, and as such I am very grateful for how willingly and sincerely the participants took on this part of the project. For the back side of the work the directive was much more open: 'Make it gold.' As anticipated, the result was that the back looked very eclectic, like a friendship quilt."

burdensome clinical view overtakes their understanding of her, blunting their imaginations.

Before they hold her in their arms, this clinical picture of their daughter supplants the experience of holding and beholding her that begins the relationship of mutual recognition between parents and their child. Such face-to-face encounters between humans, philosopher Emmanuel Levinas tells us, ground our moral relations and establish our bonds of recognition and solidarity. Only through this direct embodied encounter does the kind of human solidarity that binds families and communities together take hold. Although a mother begins to know her child during gestation, the face-to-face bond that holding and beholding her baby forges is less vulnerable to the interrupting abstraction of a diagnosis. We are most capable of loving particular human beings, distinct persons whose tender faces and fragile bodies we directly encounter.

To love is the act of recognizing one another, of witnessing the uniqueness of distinct human beings, precious and irreplaceable. The denial of a face-to-face encounter with her parents reduced that girl to one pathologized characteristic. The clinical image of that girl with the body like mine and my friends' overtook her whole being, blunting the generosity recognition brings. The static fact of her diagnosis overwhelmed other versions of how she might have lived, who she might have been, and how we might all have loved her.

The girl who is not in the world had the same potential for living a good life as any of us. Although some disabled people must live in an unwelcoming social and built environment, our disabled bodies and minds do not necessarily determine our quality of life or our prospects. What determines human flourishing is not whether a person lives with a disability but whether she is sustained by an environment of fellow humans and their offerings of resources and care. We all need to live in an environment that supports the needs of our bodies, minds, and souls. That girl with

a body like mine might have lived with dignity, surrounded by strong relationships, sustained by an accessible environment, supported by adequate economic resources, and embraced by a just and accommodating community.

How can we reimagine the life lived by this girl who is no longer in the world? How can we understand the terrible freedom her parents acted on, believing it would spare her suffering? How can we challenge the quality-of-life statistics that her medical diagnosis and other utilitarian calculations predicted? On what grounds can we offer a different "loving decision" that would welcome her among us? How can loving her differently than they did come to be a tenable, freely chosen option for her loving parents?

To make a different "loving decision" in support of their daughter's existence and her right to an open future, her parents might have turned to a literature of welcome, largely absent in the closed environment of the clinic. The modern dilemma of spiritual isolation from one another – and perhaps from the divine – has been taken up by a range of thinkers whose writings might have enabled the parents of the girl who is not in the world to reimagine their daughter, her life, and how they might have loved her in a different way. These writings clarify concepts and practices such as dignity, attention, recognition, distinctiveness, justice, equality, community, and love. They speak of universal and equal human dignity by extending the Christian tradition of *imago Dei,* being made in the image of God – a reverence for life that welcomes people with bodies like ours and hers.

This literature of welcome stretches far back in the shared wisdom traditions of our world. In modern times, philosopher Hannah Arendt reawakened an attitude of welcome at a time of great human reckoning. As a witness to the Holocaust and a victim of its hatred, Arendt repudiates the injustices that the toxic merger of eugenic ideology and totalitarianism brought to the world.

"Political regimes ought not to determine who should and who should not inhabit the world," she proclaimed in her 1963 report on the trial of Adolf Eichmann. Arendt recognizes that the eugenic regimes of the twentieth century foreclosed on human diversity and potentiality. She defies moral hierarchies based on both ancient tribalism and modern medical science. Covenants such as the Universal Declaration of Human Rights and the various equality movements, laws, and practices that sought to strengthen human justice responded to these violent moral affronts similarly. They were nascent welcoming gestures of a chastened human community, one that insisted we must, under all circumstances, recognize each other in equal dignity, despite how alien we may seem to one another.

In the wake of the Holocaust, Arendt argued that our human condition centers not on the shared mortality that we have so relentlessly imposed on one another across human history, but in our shared natality, the solidarity we might forge by recognizing that we all share birth before we share death. For Arendt, the call to human solidarity that our shared natality prompts is *Amo: volo ut sis*: "I love you: I want you to be." It appears in her post-humously published lecture "Willing." Like Levinas in his call to recognize the face of the person in front of us, Arendt proposes an ethics of nearness, inviting others into the human community and charging us to offer inclusion to all people, bound by the shared experience of being born. An attitude of welcoming attentiveness rather than ownership is the proper relation between members of the human community, particularly between parents and children. The welcoming call of natality recognizes that the solidarity amid diversity that constitutes unequivocal equality is the premise of membership in our human community. With this desire for others to be, Arendt offers the freedom to choose stewardship over selection as a model of parental love.

Arendt's natality welcomes the child at the moment of birth. Levinas's beholding assumes another whose face is already visible. The face of the girl with the body like ours was hidden from her parents at the time they made their "loving decision" to spare her from what they imagined as a life of suffering. Their reproductive

---

In the array of information presented to this girl's parents, was a meaningful vision of her as a beloved, distinctive, embodied person offered?

---

decision-making circumstance denied them the chance to behold her face, hold her in their arms, and know her in her distinctive, fully human form. In the array of information presented to this girl's parents, was a meaningful vision of her as a beloved, distinctive, embodied person offered? Their loving decision cost them both their daughter and their chance to offer her the friendship we might all extend to one another as a welcome into the world.

Where for those parents was a group of women like my friends: women with bodies like their daughter's, who befriend each other and who live good lives? The girl's parents were abandoned in their terrible freedom to choose whether to bring their daughter into the world with the body she had, to grow as she might – and for them to recognize her as theirs. What keeps me awake at night is wondering how my friends and I might accompany such abandoned parents, how we can help them behold her in a different loving way, to join with them in extending to their daughter the welcoming greeting that we all owe to each other. ⤳

ROBERT DONNELLY

# When Thousands Seek Asylum

Who are the migrants crossing
the southern US border?

# Cibola

IT'S JUST BEFORE CHRISTMAS at Cibola County Correctional Center in western New Mexico, when all eyes veer to the kid slouched in the gray bucket chair, his oversized work jacket the bright orange of a traffic cone. "*Ándale, Nacho,*" a voice squeaks to my right. All eyes now pivot toward a peach-fuzzed teen in the same thick uniform, and he squirms. "*Ándale, enseñales tu rap,*" he says.

Nacho taps together the toes of his black Crocs, the rubber slip-ons all the detained asylum seekers must wear. Black bangs swish coolly over his eyes. "*Sale,* OK," he says, and launches into a rap that's bawdy and fresh. It's a clever albeit shocking rhyme about cognac and a party girl who goes "wild" when she drinks it.

The visitors' room erupts. Peals of laughter enliven a space otherwise resembling a supermarket breakroom. A TV-VCR combo sits in an impossibly high corner of the ceiling, and even the remote is locked down in a little metal cage. Bright fluorescence shines on bulletin boards swathed in government legalese.

I'm stunned by Nacho's bravado and his rap's R-rated lyrics. Apart from me, the handful of volunteers who've come to ring in the season are middle-aged women from the Albuquerque suburbs. But I'm also impressed at how well he's mimicked the synthetic vibrato and sustain of the song. "*Cuando tome Henness-ss-sss-ssss-y,*" he mock-autotunes, stretching out and chopping the line like a scratched CD on hissy repeat.

Order soon resumes. They're good kids, after all, and probably don't want to jeopardize the alteration to routine our monthly visits afford them. This is true, I suspect, even though the activities we offer – a variation on Simon Says, origami, a birthday-guessing game, chair yoga – are more apt for either a much younger or much older crowd. Still, the smiles and laughter feel genuine, and I believe it when they tell us they're glad we've come.

Pat Bonilla, a former ESL instructor who's lived in Mexico, Ecuador, and Brazil, gets things back on track, leading everybody in a popular – and tame – villancico, "*El burrito de Belén,*" or "The Little Donkey of Bethlehem." As she sings, the guys join in, beaming and stomping their feet, clapping along, and shouting out the refrain: "*Si me ven, si me ven, voy camino de Belén.*" It's a moment. They've gotten to raise their voices and not get in trouble.

As the carol winds down, the leader of our volunteer group, Kelly McCloskey-Romero, darts a glance at her wrist. We only get an hour with the men, and learning about the conditions they face is the main reason for our visit. But she stresses another purpose of our being here: to show them there are Americans who care.

AT THIS STAGE, a Nicaraguan named Bayron emerges as the group's unofficial spokesman. At two months, he's been at Cibola longer than the rest, but, verging on thirty, he also stands up straighter and more squarely, with a gravitas absent from the youngsters around him.

Bayron's words fit a pattern we hear on other visits. The men have had their phone privileges cut, often for petty infractions, which has isolated them from family back home and potential legal allies here. There's also something called the "icebox," or *hielera*, a solitary-confinement punishment cell set at near-freezing temperatures. Medical care is deficient, Bayron adds, pointing to the case of a Dominican man who has been suffering for some time from delirium and hallucinations.

As Bayron enumerates grievances, I sense a perverse rationale. The facility's rules seem to uphold the letter of the law. The food the men get may check an official box for daily dietary needs,

---

*Robert Donnelly is a freelance writer based in Albuquerque, New Mexico.*

but, Bayron says, sometimes the potatoes are raw and the meat so packed with chili pepper it's inedible. Similarly, scalding hot water, which the men complain they can't shower with lest they burn themselves, may satisfy a legal requirement for the provision of a basic necessity. But it's also clear that such tactics represent a subtle form of punishment.

For years, such grievances have fueled human-rights accusations against officials at Cibola and Torrance, the other major detention center for asylum seekers in southeastern New Mexico. The charges, filed by the ACLU and the New Mexico Immigrant Law Center, allege rotten healthcare, aggressive guards, and official treatment ranging from negligence to abuse. Of course, such charges are common to many prisons in the United States; if anything, the legal complaints underscore how similar conditions are for asylum seekers and convicted criminals.

Yet when the twenty-two young men – twelve Venezuelans, one Nicaraguan, and two or three each from Guatemala, Ecuador, Honduras, and Colombia – file out after an hour or so, there are no shackles or handcuffs or fuming guards, and no segregation by nationality. Far from their real

Jorge Cocco Santángelo, from the series *I Was a Stranger*, oil on canvas, 2017.

families, they linger in their farewells, waving, smiling, and thanking with a gentleness belying the raucousness of Nacho's rap a few minutes before.

Outside, coils of concertina wire crown three concentric loops of stadium fencing. Jagged barbs glint like a million shiny razorblades in the bright, high-desert morning. A company flag with a boxy crimson-and-navy logo like a storage unit facility's flaps at the entrance. On the path to the guardhouse, someone has planted rosebushes, but it's months before spring, and all that's showing are thorns and skinny green stems.

Some months later, Bayron writes me from Cibola to share the frustration he's felt over the past year. Hoping to work and start a new life, he's instead been incarcerated, while a relative who had agreed to sponsor him ended up reneging. Finally getting a deportation order hasn't brought relief, since he doesn't know when the order will go through. The uncertainty this creates is a widespread concern. In 2022, a twenty-three-year-old Brazilian asylum seeker named Kesley Vial committed suicide at Torrance after repeated postponement of his deportation.

Bayron is apprehensive about setting foot in his native Nicaragua. As someone who has claimed political persecution, a typical first step in applying for asylum, he fears reprisal from the left-authoritarian government of Daniel Ortega. "They did not give me the opportunity," he writes, "to get my family out of Nicaragua. . . . I will have to once again confront the harshness of the dictatorship of my country."

The next time we exchange messages, about three months after his deportation, he sends me a photo. It shows him beaming and clutching his toddler son and slightly older daughter. He's working in construction in the Nicaraguan capital, Managua, to provide for them. He has no plans to return to the United States anytime soon.

**From the artist:** When I decided to work on the series of paintings *I Was a Stranger*, my purpose was not to chronicle an event, past or present. My main idea is to express a human drama, individual and collective, and perhaps help people gain more sensibility toward our brothers and sisters in the human race. I named this series in reference to the words of the Savior cited in Matthew 25:33–40: "I was a stranger, and ye took me in. . . ."

To convey some of the feelings a stranger might go through, I used geometric blocks, with a number of human figures all boxed together, some more realistic and some more abstract. The reality in which we live can be so daunting at times that everything seems abstract. These paintings interpret uncertainty, no sky or heavens, no progress, no front, no back, no future, no past. These are the feelings of the strangers.

Another idea I demonstrated by boxing the strangers together is that people unite and form one compact, consolidated group when they share the same experiences. They react with more empathy as they are affected by an extreme situation. The individual human shapes almost melt into a new, larger entity. The group is reduced to one small place. The rest of the space is great and abstract, not understood, not comprehended. They are surrounded by no one and nothing; they only have each other. Will we stay immobile or will we be moved to action?

—*Jorge Cocco Santángelo*

## Torrance

THE SUNRISE GLARE IS BLINDING as we zip past chalky red cliffs and mesas and pass on to scrubby prairie so open the sky is a dome stretching to the earth's curve. Ice and snow cling to roadside brush as we head to the visitors' room at Torrance.

At one end of the room a composite fresco covers a cinderblock wall, showing a mix of New Mexican landscapes: alpine firs with big-antlered elk; a snowy mountain, its flanks indigo at sunset;

the iconic Llano Estacado; a river. The painting honors those who came to this land and took ownership of it. A goateed, dark-haired soldier with a crested helmet and suit of armor is given pride of place. Next to him, a hatted, blue-eyed man gazes out with Charlton Heston intensity over the nature scenes below. In a small frame on the opposite wall, as if in afterthought, an indigenous woman contemplates a bush with violet thistles.

It's a commonplace that each wave of immigration is first vilified, then exploited, and finally welcomed. As the taint of the stranger fades, new

Jorge Cocco Santángelo, from the series *I Was a Stranger*, oil on canvas, 2017.

stories emerge to explain away inconsistencies in the record. Exaggerations on an immigration form and fabricated family connections are rationalized then mythologized, white lies to hasten the process of becoming American, with citizenship the reward for the audacity.

The young men in the room today might just mirror those earlier generations. Ostensibly, they are asylum seekers fleeing persecution. But many of them are rational opportunists, making the best of the circumstances fate has dealt them. Take the Venezuelans, for example, who account for half of the guys we routinely meet. From 2013 to 2021, when the kids in this room were in their formative teen years, the country posted double-digit GDP losses every year, with hyperinflation peaking at 130,000 percent in 2018. According to the Council on Foreign Relations, since 2014 more than eight million people have fled the country, with over 545,000 coming to the United States. Who wouldn't consider escaping such a situation?

Yet when Kelly splits us into groups, I'm surprised the men sidestep conversations about the alleged persecution they face back home – persecution that, properly articulated to a judge or case officer, could qualify them for asylum. Why don't they practice the "credible fear" rap they'll surely have to give at their hearing or interview?

But they don't. Perhaps that's because of this open-plan room and the lack of confidentiality, or because we've not gained their trust. Maybe the cause of their persecution back home was a stigmatized identity such as homosexuality – information that shouldn't be divulged in prison.

Instead, what the men want to discuss is work, their trades, and where they hope to land. One tells us he is eager to get to Houston to find work as a gardener, another to join a body shop there. A man from Guatemala says he hopes to secure a job at the McDonald's his brother works at in Connecticut, while a baker from Honduras wants to get to Phoenix. A welder from coastal Venezuela is keen to find work in Michigan.

As Kelly unfurls a laminated map of the United States, the men gather around to marvel at the expansiveness of the country, perhaps dreaming of where they might go, if they ever get the chance. Some with family in the country locate where they're living, and we volunteers point out our birthplaces.

Carlos is the most charismatic of today's eleven detainees. Along with a fellow Venezuelan, Daniel, who once had a white-collar position in a state-owned oil company, he emerges as an unofficial spokesman. While Daniel's delivery is deliberate, Carlos is effusive. "For the first time since I've been here, I've laughed and smiled," he compliments us.

I ask Carlos about his prospects. He's hopeful he'll land on his feet, but is vague about where he plans to go, not seeming to know exactly where his sponsor, a contractor in Florida, is. What surprises me more, though, is the date he gives me for his asylum hearing. "It's on the 27th, then?" I repeat. But I've misheard. "No, it's in 2027!" he says.

I'm still incredulous at this when Carlos asks if he can work in the meanwhile. "I don't know," I tell him – we've been coached to deflect requests for legal advice. I wonder, though, how anyone but the very rich could survive so long without work.

A MONTH OR SO LATER I learn that Carlos made his way to Florida, but then we lose touch. I do stay in contact with Daniel. After leaving Torrance, he has wound up in Athens, Georgia, where his sponsor lives. The quintessential southern college town is also where Laken Riley, a nursing student, was murdered by an undocumented Venezuelan border-crosser in February 2024. Her death fueled anti-immigrant polemics nationwide.

Some months afterward, I phone Daniel to ask how he's doing and if he's experienced any backlash from the killing. "*Todo tranquilo,*" he

says, as a screen door slams and cicadas buzz in the background. "I feel good. I have the *permiso* from ICE. I have the *permiso* from the court. That doesn't affect me. I'm legal."

I'm glad Daniel is not worried about retaliatory violence. Instead, he says, he's focused on more prosaic concerns: rent, food, work. Right now, he's unable to pay the $300 in attorney's fees he says he needs to apply for a work permit. The authorization is crucial. Without a job, how will he feed himself when his asylum hearing also isn't slated until 2027?

After hanging up, I wonder about Daniel's decision to emigrate. His closest relative, his daughter, is thousands of miles away. He can't legally work yet. It's unclear whether his sponsor is reliable. And his asylum hearing, a daunting three years from now, could go either way.

The social science literature indicates that immigrants are different from the rest of us. Compared with the general population, they are more likely to possess those qualities especially rewarded by the labor market: ambition, drive, work ethic, and intelligence. This is a common

Jorge Cocco Santángelo, from the series *I Was a Stranger*, oil on canvas, 2017.

refrain in the paeans Americans make to our bold, tough, and smart forebears. But what other qualities do they share? Are migrants less tolerant of their present circumstances? More likely to believe that something better lies just over the horizon?

It's a chilly December morning at a chain hotel near the Albuquerque International Sunport. I'm here to pick up a Venezuelan family of asylum seekers whom a local charity has put up. Like many, they crossed at Ciudad Juárez, Mexico, before requesting asylum in El Paso, Texas. Yesterday they took a bus from the border and now they're flying to Kentucky, where sponsors have agreed to host them. I'm to escort them to their gate.

Carla, the family's twelve-year-old daughter, is showing off the new mall clothes the charity has bought her: a purse, crisp slacks, a white blouse with ruffles. She can hardly contain herself. Long curly brown hair frames a face frequently lit up by bright, candid smiles.

Geidy, the mother, tells me of the danger and risk the family endured on their journey to arrive here. She describes a hopscotch-like set of jumps, first west to Colombia, then south to Chile, and finally north to the United States. All told, the family has been on the road for four years. Like her daughter, Geidy is also wearing a brand-new outfit, with one additional accessory: an electronic monitoring device, courtesy of ICE, Velcroed to her left ankle – something I notice as she's putting her shoes back on after the security check.

Carlos, the father, tells me that the most nerve-wracking stretch of their journey was through the Darién Gap, the remote jungle region straddling northern Colombia and southern Panama. Poor migrants with no other choice form ad hoc bands, then hike for days through marshes and mountain passes. Human bones are a common sight on the trek.

Carlos shifts closer to show me photos on his phone: migrants, bundled against the wind and cold, flash grins and make hand signs from atop moving trains in Mexico. There are many women and girls among them, even a toddler in a pink coat. The images are unexpectedly cheerful, given that so many migrants call Mexico the most dangerous and violent country on the journey. When I first started airport escort a few years ago, two Cuban women confided that they'd been held for months near the Mexican city of Monterrey while their families in Florida arranged ransom payments to secure their release.

Knowing this, I wonder why Geidy and Carlos risked traveling from Chile through the Darién Gap and up the length of Mexico with their preteen daughter. "Why didn't you just stay in Chile?" I ask. Carlos mumbles something about Geidy's family being in Kentucky and how Chileans are "*gris*," or boring. But I still have a hard time understanding. Chile is no Venezuela. It's politically stable, and from what I gather, Geidy and Carlos's economic position was OK. They both had jobs there, and Geidy, who worked as a maid, shows me photos of a trip she took with her boss to Valparaíso, a Chilean beach resort.

But there's no time for more questions as the gate agent calls their boarding group, so we hug and exchange contact information. They're happy to finally be on the very last leg of their journey. A week or so later, I check in with Geidy on WhatsApp. Her profile picture now shows a living room with a dressed Christmas tree. Through the room's parted curtains, snow falls on a lawn. "Merry Christmas from Louisville," it says.

# Deming

It's a blazing hot southwestern spring day. Green shoots fringe the banks of the Rio Grande as it meanders south. Waves of heat and exhaust rise from the nearby interstate as rigs rumble toward Los Angeles or Jacksonville.

Ariana Saludares grew up here in New Mexico. Today, she helps run Colores United, a nonprofit serving refugees and asylum seekers. We meet at the group's shelter in Deming, a small town thirty-six miles from the border. Apart from Saludares and her children, Jack and Caia, the rambling, one-story building – an erstwhile motorcycle shop with corrugated white aluminum siding whose original sign still sits atop a pole outside – is empty. Saludares has given the volunteers, mostly local moms, time off to recharge.

But the break is also for planning the shelter's next chapter: a move later this year to a ranch in the countryside. There, near the otherwise inhospitable desert, migrants from Turkey, Cuba, Brazil, and elsewhere will finally get to exhale. "We're more of a respite than a shelter," Saludares says, as we tour the new site, a thirty-acre former pecan farm. "We first want to help people heal emotionally as they make the last leg of their journey. What does that look like? *Descansar, comer, dormir.* A warm bed, a hot meal, a good night's sleep."

Saludares plans to build stables for equine therapy, and wooden dinosaur replicas on which kids can climb and play. Woods with deer, squirrels, woodpeckers, and quail will foster a sense of peace. "People will be coming off the worst three to six months of their lives (both in transit and in custody)," Saludares says, as we pause in the shade of a cedar tree. "So we choose just to give them space. I can't change their experience in detention, but I can change the experience they have here."

The shelter's inconspicuous location has an added benefit. Away from town, it's more insulated from Colores United's political enemies, who, Saludares says, have insulted her on Facebook, told her, "Go back to where you come from," and threatened to "bury you in the desert." "My family is extremely concerned," she tells me. "The far right are not very happy with

what nonprofit organizations are doing with immigrants." A shelter in San Diego, California, recently had a prominent online provocateur show up posing as a pest exterminator, while in Texas the state attorney general is actively trying to shut down several leading faith-based service providers, claiming they encourage illegal immigration.

To cope with the hostility, Saludares has staked a low profile for the organization while at the same time constructively engaging some of her critics' concerns. For example, she's tried to allay perceptions that migrants overuse community resources by opening the nonprofit's food pantry and discount clothing store to all the area's residents.

Like similar facilities along the border, the ranch is meant to be a temporary stop. Qualified asylum seekers will stay a short time before transitioning into permanent housing, generally under the roof of the citizen or legal resident sponsoring their case. Besides a place to sleep, the shelter will provide meals and basic healthcare, with space for about a hundred people at a time. For its part, Colores United will be eligible for reimbursement for those in its care, thanks to an $800,000 allocation in 2024 from the Federal Emergency Management Agency's Shelter and Services Program.

Colores United is not religiously affiliated, and Saludares uses the term "interfaith" loosely to describe its orientation. "Even if we don't identify with a single faith, it doesn't mean we're all not spiritual," she says, adding that it's common at the downtown shelter for guests to say grace before communally served meals, and that many volunteers belong to local churches.

In explaining the shelter's mission, Saludares strikes a balance. On the one hand, it carries out a vital humanitarian duty, particularly in its care of women and children. On the other, it has an important public safety function, since it ensures a secure, central location for authorities to bring asylum seekers when detention facilities can't hold them.

Otherwise, migrants might get dumped on the streets with no place to go, becoming easy prey for sex traffickers and other criminal elements. "Our community is safer when we take care of these individuals," Saludares says. "If they are on the street, then the traffickers come, the coyotes come."

SALUDARES'S OWN JOURNEY to this point was circuitous. After leaving home she did stints in Arizona and the Pacific Northwest, where she soured on a career in luxury property management – "It's frivolous," she says. It was in Sicily, while her husband was stationed at a US Navy air base, that she discovered her calling.

It was the height of the Syrian civil war, with thousands fleeing daily aboard rickety boats in the Mediterranean. "There were refugees all over Sicily," Saludares says. "I would keep oranges in my car to give away." She was intensely moved by the image shared around the world of a little boy in a red shirt and blue pants washed up like flotsam on a Turkish beach.

While Saludares talks, I look at her twelve-year-old son, who, with his coppery tan and sun-streaked mop of hair, looks like he belongs on the cover of a skateboarding magazine. Refreshingly, he's entertaining himself without a phone, alternating between bouncing a ping-pong ball on the downtown shelter's cement floor and jerking the controls of a vintage Pac-Man arcade game. He's around the same age the boy in the photo, Alan Kurdi, would be had he lived.

"I stay awake at night thinking about the children who migrate," she says. "A child doesn't make the decision to walk the Darién Gap. After seeing that photo, I knew I had to do something."

In 2019 Saludares got her chance when a major surge brought thousands of asylum seekers to Deming. With a population of just fifteen thousand, the town's resources quickly dwindled, and, in May, authorities declared a state of emergency in a bid to unlock federal and state help. They also called on nonprofits and churches to house migrants temporarily while cases wound through the courts.

But, located less than an hour from Mexico, this is a small community where migration politics hit hard and many see large numbers of even legal, asylum-seeking individuals as something like an invasion. Border Patrol and Customs and Border Protection have an outsized presence here, with some five hundred officers and agents and their families living in the area.

The politics were daunting, Saludares says. Some townsfolk grew resentful, believing that new arrivals overused local resources while needy citizens went without. Others argued that charities such as Colores United fueled even more migration by offering incentives for asylum seekers to cross the border. The upshot: impoverished frontline communities unable to cope. "It was so polarized, with some Deming folks wanting to help, others opposed," Saludares says.

Five years on, the situation seems more balanced. Authorities are no longer releasing over one hundred migrants at a time onto downtown streets. And those who fear migrants will overuse scant resources seem less vocal. This is thanks to the shelter's success in moving people on, she says, but also to the organization's efforts to serve the wider community.

I ask Saludares how recent policy developments, such as the government's decision to drastically limit the number of asylum seekers, will affect her work. She tells me she doesn't think the overall volume of migrants will drop, but that the balance will simply shift, with more people attempting to enter undocumented if fewer people can apply for asylum. "Migration is never going to go away," she says. "You can build a hundred-foot wall, but people with a mission will always make it, no matter. People don't come all this way to just turn around and head back south." ⇒

# And Is It Not Enough?

And is it not enough that every year
A richly laden autumn should unfold
And shimmer into being leaf by leaf,
Its scattered ochres mirrored everywhere
In hints and glints of hidden red and gold
Threaded like memory through loss and grief,

When dusk descends, when branches are unveiled,
When roots reach deeper than our minds can feel
And ready us for winter with strange calm,
That I should see the inner tree revealed
And know its beauty as the bright leaves fall
And feel its truth within me as I am?

And is it not enough that I should walk
Through low November mist along the bank,
When scents of woodsmoke summon, in some long
And melancholy undertone, the talk
Of those old poets from whose works I drank
The heady wine of an autumnal song?

It is not yet enough. So I must try,
In my poor turn, to help you see it too,
As though these leaves could be as rich as those,
That red and gold might glimmer in your eye,
That autumn might unfold again in you,
Feeling with me what falling leaves disclose.

*MALCOLM GUITE*

From *Parable and Paradox*, copyright © 2016 by Malcolm Guite,
published by Canterbury Press and reproduced by permission
of Hymns Ancient & Modern Ltd. All rights reserved.

# A Lion in Phnom Penh

An insider reckons with
complicity and compromise
in Cambodia's aid industry.

**J. DANIEL SIMS**

THE BRIGHT, THICK TROPICAL SUN filters yellow through the fading canvas outside Lone Pine Café on Phnom Penh's busy Pasteur Street. *Tuk tuks*, motorbikes, and a shocking number of exotic sports cars whir outside.

The proprietor is an old-timer, a former award-winning midtown Manhattan restaurateur who cashed out in the early aughts. He moved here to fade softly into a different sort of concrete jungle. The food business, though, was in his blood, and he couldn't resist one last venture. Decor is certainly not the appeal of the aging Cali-Mex dive. Patrons flock to rumors of the best margaritas and burritos this side of the Mekong. They stay because the rumors are very true – but also because Lone Pine Café is just the sort of dimly lit watering hole where certain stories can still be whispered at the ragged edge of an authoritarian state.

THIS PARTICULAR STORY starts simply enough. Somewhere in the United Nations' sprawling Cambodia mission exists a certain "protection officer." Her core responsibility is to monitor Cambodia's "rehabilitation" shelters and ultimately decide whether her agency should continue to fund and support them.

On a site visit with other observers, what she found was not a shelter at all, but a prison. Upon entering, she was hit with the overwhelming odor of trash and human waste. The little light inside was a dingy and ominous gray. Only the oppressive heat of the equatorial sun effectively penetrated the windowless concrete walls. Living quarters were cramped. Food rations were minimal and foul.

The protection officer observed sick and malnourished "patients," a man lying semiconscious and unattended (who later died), and a woman going into labor with no medical support. The United Nations holds a strong rhetorical stance on the dignity of vulnerable individuals. Since a UN agency was providing direct funding

support to the ministry overseeing the shelter, one might have expected it to respond vigorously to its agent's witness of gross neglect.

Yet the impact of this site visit – like so many others – was nil. A tidy list of recommendations was provided to the overseeing ministry. Some nonbinding guidance was offered to improve management of the facility, and the list was dutifully accepted, stamped, filed, and ignored by the ministry. Funding continued and no public condemnations were issued about the conditions found at this shelter. Nothing changed.

This facility is a fairly representative example of Cambodia's government-run shelters. Of the myriad humanitarian and human-rights crises festering within Cambodia's borders, such places rank among the worst.[1]

According to Sebastian Strangio's book *Cambodia: From Pol Pot to Hun Sen and Beyond*, these shelters are widely used as holding places for undesirables. Drug addicts and street people are rounded up "typically in accelerated fashion prior to visits from foreign dignitaries." As one municipal government official summed up, if world leaders "see beggars and children on the street, they might speak negatively to and about the government."

Despite the existence of some reporting on these shelters, their true condition is not widely acknowledged. This represents a defining feature of the aid industry one might call an "engagement imperative." This imperative is an unspoken set of incentives to prioritize relations between the "partners" (foreign watchdogs, international organizations, NGOs, and the like) and "host government" entities.

The dominant perspective within the Western aid world holds that humanitarian goals are most effectively pursued with the cooperation of local institutions. This is a rational operating assumption. Without a deep level of engagement with

1. "Death in Prey Speu Highlights Detention Center Abuses," Cambodian League for the Promotion and Defense of Human Rights (website), Dec. 7, 2014.

the host government, most aid groups would be unable to carry out their programs – programs designed to reach the most vulnerable.

But this imperative to work within the system necessitates significant moral tradeoffs. Reasonable arguments may be made for where the cost of engagement outweighs the benefit, where to draw the line. Beyond such utilitarian analysis, though, the habits formed by repeatedly engaging in such tradeoffs render them difficult to see at all. Fundamentally, an industry that aligns itself with state power (and the money that comes with it) has every reason *not* to recognize the negative effects of that alignment.

Yet, beyond "the industry" itself as a bogeyman – and notwithstanding the many dedicated individuals working earnestly in this space – Cambodia is rife with sickening stories of aid-worker hypocrisy.

There are the human rights advocates who are meant to be protecting the poor from land grabs but instead play golf with corrupt officials on stolen land; environmental activists with big SUVs in their driveways and rosewood furniture in their homes; NGO leaders ensuring their own comfort and security while sustaining corrupt and predatory elites.

Such stories have the potential to open our eyes to the insufficiency of powerful systems to address human need. We could take them as humbling reminders of individual fallibility and doublethink.

Or we could dismiss these stories and their tellers, labeling as "cynical" that which is merely a matter of historical record.

Or perhaps worse, we could allow the darkness of such stories to instill in us a smug sense of somehow being better or more holy or more altruistic or more pure. That, if only it were "us" calling the shots, everything would be very different.

So let me be clear: this story could just as easily be about me. And indeed it is.

"SIR, YOUR FUNDS are now frozen per guidance from the United States Office of Foreign Assets Control."

These are never the words you want to hear as you are wrapping up a frantic Target run with your eight-month-old daughter. And, let me assure you, they are certainly not the words your wife wants to hear as she steels herself for the pandemic-enhanced gauntlet of boarding an overseas flight in 2021.

*But why?*

The Office of Foreign Assets Control (OFAC), to me, harks back to episodes of *Narcos*, *24*, or *The Sopranos* – one of many arms in the US government's fight against drugs, terrorism, organized crime, and the like. Founded in 1950, its mission was largely driven by Cold War geopolitics up to the fall of the Soviet Union. Since then, the ballooning aid industry has become, like OFAC, one more tool for the promotion of liberal democratic ideals and "fair play" capitalism the world over. Freedom, by a certain definition.

To the likes of OFAC, I was one of the good guys. My résumé rang out like a love ballad to progressive idealism: supporting pro-democracy rebel groups and reporting on human rights abuses in northern Myanmar; establishing a "win-win social enterprise" in post-conflict Uganda; and leading "evidence-informed" policy research at a prestigious American university. And now, as China's shadow loomed over the region, I was out pushing a rule-of-law agenda for a prominent NGO in one of the most corrupt and pro-Beijing countries on the planet.[2]

If those aren't pro-democracy bonafides, I don't

2. See entry for Cambodia on WJP Rule of Law Index, World Justice Project (website).

---

*J. Daniel Sims works to combat transnational crime and rights abuses in Southeast Asia and serves as a formal advisor to leading international organizations in the sector. His analysis has appeared in the* New York Times, Washington Post, BBC, *and the* Economist.

*Previous spread:* photograph by Roman Koenig, from his series *Glimpses of the Slums of Phnom Penh*, Cambodia, 2021–22.

know what is. *So, what in the world did Uncle Sam want with my petty savings accounts?* The answer to that question goes back fourteen years, to a small Cambodian village experiencing a very different side of "freedom" and "progress."

Not much changed for the people of Lor Peang as Cambodia's civil war died down in the late 1980s. The Soviets moved on and the UN peacekeepers arrived to usher in a new era. Sure, they saw the Land Cruisers come in and heard the foreigners preach to them about democracy. An election was held, and they courageously cast their ballots, despite the risk of doing so. When the party aligned with the old monarchy was named the victor, it seemed to promise stability. But it soon became clear that Hun Sen's Cambodian People's Party would not accept the outcome.

Not much changed for Lor Peang in 1996, when a significant portion of the village was reclassified as the Ta Ches Commune Special Economic Zone (SEZ). In theory, SEZs facilitate rapid economic growth through tax incentives to attract foreign investment and spark technological advancement. In Cambodia, they have historically served as vehicles for speculation and land-grabbing by members of the ruling elite. Today, they are increasingly used as havens for organized crime, human exploitation, and elite-driven lawlessness writ large.[3] But still, not much changed in Lor Peang, for a while.

It was November 9, 2007, when the bulldozers rolled into this quiet little village forty miles north of Phnom Penh. Through some bureaucratic magic and likely backroom deals with provincial authorities, KDC International (a company owned by the wife of a cabinet minister) acquired the rights to this SEZ and began "productive economic engagement."[4] This engagement began and ended with plowing down a number of homes

in the village and erecting a fence around the perimeter. Meanwhile, the new owners sat back and waited for real estate prices to rise.

That same year, this power couple began construction on another investment project – my future home.

It was 2020. We were moving to Cambodia in the dead of Covid winter, with a newborn. It's different looking for an apartment with a baby. The tiny amount of money you save getting a walk-up just doesn't seem worth it anymore. Every single square inch of space you can afford certainly does. You start thinking about things like security and architectural integrity and how much of the day the pool is shaded. And of course, the normal considerations – proximity to work, area quality, and whether the neighbors are sane.

In Cambodia, to have it all – the proximity, vibe, and space, the like-minded community and fun neighborhood, the yuppie family dreamscape – Romdoul Bopha apartment complex was perfect. All for less than the price of a crummy apartment on the outskirts of DC (but exponentially more than the average price in Phnom Penh).

Romdoul was by no means the most luxurious building in the neighborhood, nor were its occupants the wealthiest. Those distinctions belonged to the children of ranking government officials and their sprawling, leafy villas, along with their endless stream of Ferraris, McLarens, Bentleys, and Rolls-Royces. So our home didn't stand out as flashy, but it attracted a certain clientele: diplomats, successful European "consultant" and "advisor" types, country directors of prominent American NGOs, and even, for a spell, the ranking UN official in Cambodia.

These folks fit our demographic to a tee. Many had young children. Few were on their first deployment – they'd been around the block a couple times. Most, if not all, saw Phnom Penh for what it is: problematic in many ways, but by no means a hardship post in the broader view of the industry.

3. *Forced to Scam: Cambodia's Cyber Slaves,* 101 East, *Al Jazeera* (2022), 46 min, available on YouTube.
4. Focus on the Global South, *Case Study Report: Lor Peang Community Land Conflict* (2018), free online.

Strangio describes expat life in Phnom Penh as "a sybaritic blur of cheap entertainment, running the gamut from panini bars and yoga classes to hip cafés, social enterprise set-ups, and cocktail happy hours. Rent and domestic help are inexpensive, internet connections are fast, and just about every sort of indulgence is imported from abroad. . . . A spell in Cambodia is generally a comfortable step on the way to somewhere else, and everybody wants to leave with a gold star on their CV."

And that about summed up our time in the Kingdom of Wonder. Until it didn't. Some months later we had more or less settled into our rhythm. We'd found some friends, gotten the hang of my job and hers, and picked out our favorite "hip" café. We took our annual home leave in the spring, and that is when it happened.

One crisp morning, I was deep into a trail run in the oh-so-non-tropical Colorado Front Range. As I rounded a rocky bend that opened up an expansive vista, I realized in a flash: we

hadn't paid our rent! One of the many oddities of our Cambodian life was that our landlords explicitly required all rent to be paid in cash. This would now be impossible as we wouldn't be back for another few weeks. I pulled out my phone and messaged the property manager, asking her how to proceed. She said it was fine to wait, but I insisted. We wanted to pay now. Eventually, she forwarded wire instructions. I submitted the transfer when I got home and thought nothing of it until the call from my bank about the Office of Foreign Assets Control. A suspicious transfer had apparently put me on the agency's radar.

I submitted an appeal through my bank and attested to the purpose of the transfer and my lack of knowledge of the situation. I stressed – with extra credibility – what exactly I was doing in Cambodia. *I'm one of the good guys. You definitely don't want to hold on to my money. Those funds are the ones that help me do the good stuff!*

And seemingly, it worked. Actually, I'm not sure

Photograph by Roman Koenig, from his series
*Glimpses of the Slums of Phnom Penh*, Cambodia, 2021–22.

what happened. No one ever confirmed whether my transaction was in violation of any sort of statute. In any case, within a few weeks, our funds were unlocked. We returned to Cambodia and resumed paying our – potentially illicit – rent in cash. Always in cash.

But it also sparked my curiosity about why our landlords, a married couple, were apparently blacklisted. I knew the husband was the Minister of Mines and Energy. That status certainly hadn't resulted in a cut to our electricity bill, and I had not given it much further thought.

What I found upon a bit more digging shocked me.

The wife was the head of KDC International – the perpetrator of the Lor Peang land grab. This was one of the most famous land grabs in a country where hundreds of thousands were similarly stripped of their property and a small elite amassed a fortune through state-sanctioned theft. Yet Lor Peang wasn't the biggest or the

most violent or even the one most directly linked to abuses of government power. Rather, it was famous because the displaced people had had the nerve to fight back. Nonviolent protests had attracted some minor attention among (mostly local) human rights groups. A pittance was offered to a few of the displaced villagers, while many more were jailed for their willingness to speak up.

Some reports suggested the wife had also been involved in orphan trafficking – selling children to agencies[5] for adoption by rich parents in the United States and elsewhere. The husband was considered one of the more nepotistic and corrupt ministers[6] in one of the world's most corrupt governments, his ministry stocked full of his own family members and allies. He had long been suspected of skimming off the top[7] of Cambodia's

5. Bill Bainbridge, "Adoptive Parents Tell of Agency's Deception," *Phnom Penh Post,* Feb. 15, 2002.
6. *opendevelopmentcambodia.net/tag/suy-sem.*
7. Meas Sokchea, "Minister to Be Grilled on Sand Export Discrepancy," *Phnom Penh Post,* Dec. 14, 2016.

Photograph by Roman Koenig, from his series *Glimpses of the Slums of Phnom Penh,* Cambodia, 2021–22.

labyrinth of natural resource concessions to foreign direct investors. For example, in 2009, an Australian mining company paid hundreds of thousands of dollars to various members of his family residing in the United States in exchange for mineral rights.[8] The company was later convicted in the United States for wrongdoing.

According to one long-time Cambodian human rights advocate, my landlord is "easily a top three Cambodia bad guy" amid stiff competition.

My little bit of due diligence hadn't fully uncovered the reason for the blocked transfer, but it unsettled me profoundly. I felt like something needed to change, and was uncertain what it would imply for my family's future. I figured I'd informally poll my fellow Romdoulians.

"Do you know about our landlords?"

"Like what about them?"

"Like, who they really are?"

Most of the residents of Romdoul Bopha were aware he was a minister and that "they were probably corrupt." But it ended there.

"They provide a good service and a safe home for my kids, and they fix the toilet when it clogs. That's all I know," said an Aussie diplomat.

As I shared what I learned and dug deeper, the answers I got confounded me. Yet they also felt strangely familiar, and, in a way, reassuring.

"Sometimes, putting money in the pockets of people like that is a necessary evil. It is the cost of trying to do good," said an NGO advisor.

Accepting such moral ambiguities as "the cost of trying to do good" is a fundamental premise of the sector, not unrelated to the engagement imperative. And, of course, there is wisdom in such an acceptance of one's inability to achieve some sort of abstract moral purity. Yet this particular "necessary evil" is a pretty bad one. It traces its roots back to the earliest UN peacekeeping days in Cambodia, when ruling party officials started grabbing land and renting it out

at a huge premium to aid workers and diplomats. One of the key ways the regime holds power to this day is its control over revenue. And one of the key sources of revenue (then and now) is expat aid-worker rent.

I wondered: Isn't there a better way? These are exploiters and we are incentivizing their exploitative behavior on a monthly payment schedule.

"That's just how the market works. We have to live somewhere, right? If we only lived in the homes of noncorrupt people, we'd be on the outskirts in the slums where no one is fighting over land," mused a German economist.

It is true that the vast majority of public services in Cambodia would collapse if the international community pulled out. If NGOs suddenly refused to engage with the regime or stopped paying their staff enough to procure safe and secure housing, many aid workers would leave and poor Cambodians would suffer. Many would die. That's an inherent paradox of aid dependency and a cautionary note for those seeking simple solutions.

"I guess, if it doesn't sit well, you could move out there, but do you really want to do that to your family?" offered a consultant.

Of course I didn't want to do that. And indeed I did not. I continued to be the faithful do-gooder paying an abusive thief for the right to live on his property while I collected a handsome salary for my efforts to help the victims of his crimes.

I DID INVEST DEEPLY in my job with a major NGO whose purpose in this region is to fight the scourge of forced labor. We worked with Cambodian authorities to rescue victims of trafficking, pursue legal cases against traffickers and slaveholders, and train local law enforcement to identify cases of violent labor abuse It's work I deeply believe in and it's what I had come to do.

Forced labor is pervasive in Cambodia. A common story is of men who are tricked into traveling abroad to work in Thailand's enormous

8. Douglas Gillison, "OZ Minerals Deal a Windfall for Officials' Kin," *Cambodia Daily,* May 31, 2011.

fishing industry.[9] Once there, where they don't speak the language or have any meaningful protection under the law, they are among the most vulnerable people in the world.[10]

This exploitation is abetted by a legal system that has had a notoriously difficult time holding perpetrators accountable (especially powerful ones like my landlords). Forced labor also arises from limited economic opportunities and high rates of landlessness among the rural poor.[11]

---

The irony of it took my breath away. I was here to fight labor trafficking and I was enabling it to the tune of $1,300 per month plus utilities.

---

Landlessness is compounded by the microfinance sector[12] – another do-gooder industry doing harm as lenders peddle loans at usurious interest rates while holding deeds and titles as collateral. Loans mostly go to farmers who have no credible means of paying back their tiny yet existentially threatening debts. They lose their land to the banks or secondary lenders and with it their only meaningful asset or livelihood in what one recent study called an efficient "system of poor-to-rich wealth transfer."[13] Landless former farmers then have to take bigger risks to make ends meet. Many look abroad. And the cycle continues.

Landlessness also proliferates from, naturally, land grabbing.[14]

And this is the end of the story of Lor Peang, that once-peaceful village, forty miles north of my precious margaritas and safe compound with the pool that gets shade all afternoon. Kicked off their land (by my landlord) and their leaders imprisoned (by the very legal system I was here to help reform), their options were limited. A follow-up survey several years after the land grab confirmed that over ninety percent of Lor Peang's working-age men had been trafficked into the Thai fishing industry.[15]

The irony of it took my breath away. I was here to fight labor trafficking and I was enabling it to the tune of $1,300 per month plus utilities. I began to confront the reality that I was complicit in more insidious ways as well, propping up a violent system with my involvement in the symbiotic cycles of aid money and global capitalism. And I worried over the difference between my professional responsibility, which began and ended with my terms of reference and three-year contract, and my moral responsibility, which seemed to demand something more.

Whereas Western aid workers frequently struggled and failed when confronted with these moral paradoxes, local allies seemed far more clear-eyed about matters. "If you do nothing, you will still become a victim. It's just not your turn yet." These words from Cambodia's most famous rights activist sum up the worldview of those whose lives and stories and blood are bound up in this place. Such clarity comes at a high cost. Kem Ley was murdered by the ruling party shortly after uttering this defiant statement against silent complicity.[16]

Even in the face of Western paralysis, other

9. Daniel Murphy, "Hidden Chains: Rights Abuses and Forced Labor in Thailand's Fishing Industry," Human Rights Watch (website), Jan. 23, 2018.

10. Issara Institute and International Justice Mission, *Not in the Same Boat: Prevalence & Patterns of Labour Abuse Across Thailand's Diverse Fishing Industry* (2017), online.

11. United Nations Office on Drugs and Crime, *Global Report on Trafficking in Persons 2022*, online.

12. "German Government-Funded Study Confirms Grave Problems in Cambodia's Microfinance Sector," Cambodian League for the Promotion and Defense of Human Rights (website), Sept. 14, 2022.

13. Abby Seiff and Sokummono Khan, "The Danger of Microfinance: Small Loans in Cambodia Drown the Poor and Buoy the Rich," *The Dial*, no. 5, May 30, 2023.

14. Gerald Flynn and Phoung Vantha, "'What Other Country Would Do This to Its People?' Cambodian Land Grab Victims Seek Int'l Justice," Mongabay, April 1, 2021.

15. May Titthara and Derek Stout, "Young Men Face the Brunt of Land Dispute," *Phnom Penh Post*, Sept. 30, 2011.

16. "Cambodian Activists Remember 2016 Shooting of Leading Government Critic," Radio Free Asia (website), July 10, 2024.

Cambodians were courageously stepping into Kem Ley's shoes. In fact, while I stood by the pool and wrung my hands, another activist was languishing in prison merely for printing the above quote on a T-shirt.[17]

As for me, with conflicting commitments and without a clear sense of how to proceed, I didn't, and the conversations with my neighbors eventually faded into the background. All expressed some concern, but no one felt they could challenge the status quo. I started to wonder whether perhaps we were all just weak and spent humans, who simply lacked the requisite fight to "confront the system" when it came down to it.

Here again, it turned out I was wrong.

THIS IS THE PART where my story turns from the merely complex and depressing to the outright bizarre.

It wasn't long after our chats about our landlords' human rights abuses died down that a lion moved in next door.

One morning in June 2021, my Twitter feed blew up with a video appearing to show a lion pacing inside a luxury villa. Strange, yes. But stranger still, I recognized the villa adjacent to our complex. It was clear that this video was taken from a Romdoulian's balcony.

All day, the Romdoul Bopha Mafia (our building's WhatsApp group) was ablaze with gossip and disbelief about this new addition to the neighborhood. That evening, I walked past the villa and saw it for myself. Peering out over a small fence on the second floor was a *very large* lion. Parked right outside was the most recognizable car in the country.

In a neighborhood chock-full of flashy sports cars, this one stands out. The Lamborghini Aventador SVJ is in a very small class of hyper-exclusive supercars, with a starting list price of over

$500,000 and a total of nine hundred units ever built. Having such a vehicle will definitely help one stand out amidst any circle of nouveau riche, bored children of the kleptocratic elite. Yet, as if that exclusivity did not suffice, this one was wrapped in a gaudy pearlized metallic finish.

Almost any Cambodian national could identify the "alleged" owner, a notorious playboy relative of the prime minister, though the words could not be said out loud. Beyond his documented penchant for violence and drug-trafficking[18] and industrial-scale scamming operations,[19] he was a known wildlife and auto aficionado. A member of the royal family also happened to be on the cadastral register of the villa. The circumstantial evidence was overwhelming. This was likely his lion.

Given how the conversations with my neighbors about our landlords were going, I expected a muted response.

Not so.

Messages poured into the group chat. "That poor animal! It deserves to be in the wild!" "Such brazen lawlessness to allow this to happen!" "What if it kills its owner? Then what?" "What if it escapes? This is not safe for *our* children!"

Within a day, someone from our building had identified a friend at the largest wildlife rescue NGO in the country and agitated for quick and effective action. By the end of the next day, the lion was gone and state-owned newspapers were reporting that the owner, "a Chinese man," had been ordered to pay a $30,000 fine.[20] Victory.

But the story didn't end there. Two days later, the prime minister made a formal announcement stating that the lion was not eating because "it missed the owner." He was making a sympathetic decision to return it to "the Chinese man" on the

---

17. Ouch Sony, "Justice Unlikely in Kem Ley T-Shirt Trial, Activist Kung Raiya Says," Voice of Democracy (website), May 20, 2020.

18. Nick McKenzie and Richard Baker, "Drugs: Our Man in Cambodia," *Sydney Morning Herald,* March 26, 2012.
19. Jack Adamović Davies, "Hun To Went After the Press; Who Really Won?" Radio Free Asia (website), July 19, 2024.
20. "Update: 'Pet Lion' Found in Phnom Penh Kept under 'Poor' Conditions and Had Teeth Removed," *Khmer Times,* June 28, 2021.

condition it was kept in a "proper cage."[21] The $30,000 fine was also, of course, magnanimously refunded.

Global media outlets picked up the story, mostly parroting the government's talking points about the supposed owner of the lion with no mention of who owned the villa where it turned up or the conspicuous sports car parked out front. Predictably, they cast the prime minister in a benevolent, if clownish, light.

This story – a case in point of corruption, nepotism, and a broken legal system that serves to oppress and exploit millions while those on top do whatever they want – was merely a meme. (To be fair, it was a pretty good meme.)

Outrage ensued at Romdoul Bopha. Of course, no cage was built, and the lion escaped a few weeks later. The prime minister weighed in on the issue again, stating that if the lion escaped again, it would be taken for good. A few weeks later, it did escape *again*. Nothing happened and there was no comment from the prime minister this time.

Yet the Romdoulians raged on. This went on for close to three months, and it seemed we had lost.

Then, one day, the lion disappeared and never returned. Just like that, it was over. Although there were probably other factors, our advocacy apparently had some sort of material and lasting impact. This collection of meek technocrats had acted outside the scope of their jobs, stood up to the most powerful person in the country, and, in a very quiet and limited way, won. The neighborhood was safer because of us. The one where *we* lived and *we* were affected.

And there we were, elated at the victorious eviction of the lion from our neighbor's yard as our own landlord used our rent checks to enforce the displacement of villagers forty miles north.

No specks here. Everyone's got a full-on plank in their eye in this town.

BY THIS POINT, increasingly disgusted by my inert complicity in larger problems than a lion, I was eager to do something more. It wasn't much, but I started by co-drafting and putting my name atop a joint statement with some local NGO leaders to sound the alarm on a new wave of human trafficking.[22]

In short, during the economic shocks of the pandemic, tens of thousands of foreign nationals were lured to Cambodia by fraudulent recruitment ads on social media, and then held against their will in militarized compounds. And these compounds weren't hidden off in the jungle. Rather, they stood in plain sight, situated in repurposed casinos, hotels, and apartment complexes in the center of Cambodia's largest cities. Public records clearly showed they were owned by powerful members of the ruling party – senators, ministers, advisors to the prime minister, and yeah, the lion guy.[23] One of the most notorious of these operated with impunity directly across the street from the prime minister's summer home.

Sophisticated criminal networks protected by the ruling elite were forcing imprisoned workers to perpetrate cyberscams against naive rich people across the globe. With workers in the compounds each generating hundreds of dollars a day in revenue, this quickly became a $12 billion per year racket – easily the largest industry in Cambodia.[24]

The situation facing activists working against this industry of state-organized crime was turning hostile.[25] Active surveillance and intimidation against the small number of groups

21. Keat Soriththeavy and Mech Dara, "Pet Lion Returned after Support for Owner, Criticism for Wildlife Center," Voice of Democracy, July 5, 2021.

22. "[Joint Statement] Abolish Slave Compounds in Cambodia," FORUM-ASIA (website), March 11, 2022.
23. "Transnational Crime in Southeast Asia: A Growing Threat to Global Peace and Security," United States Institute of Peace (website), May 13, 2024.
24. "ASEAN, China, and UNODC Agree to a Plan of Action to Address Criminal Scams in Southeast Asia," United Nations Office on Drugs and Crime (website), Sept. 26, 2023.
25. Mech Dara, "Cambodia: Chinese Human-Trafficking Rescuer Charged with Incitement amid Widespread Forced Labour of Foreign Nationals," Business & Human Rights Resource Centre (website), March 2, 2022.

engaged on the issue was mounting rapidly.[26]

International "partners" knew about the situation, but none of the other big foreign NGOs had been willing to sign on to the joint statement, due to a prevailing desire not to rock the boat. In spite of the evidence, the official Cambodian government position was a flat denial of the existence of the criminal industry, a position that went effectively unchallenged. The engagement imperative continued to rule the day.

I felt compelled to step outside these unspoken but clear boundaries and was proud to find my organization willing to stand with me as I signed on the dotted line. I hoped, perhaps idealistically, that we could use our hefty megaphone and my almighty US passport to really stand on the side of the vulnerable.

But even this sort of stand only goes so far. I was struck by how one of my Khmer friends, one

of the country's last independent journalists, saw it: "Jake, we appreciate the gesture of solidarity, but ultimately that is what it amounts to, a gesture. At the end of the day, when *they* come for you, you just leave. Then you go about your life and we remain."

It was not a condemnation. He was affirming that I'd done the right thing and perhaps even an unusual thing for someone in my shoes. Such abstract "gestures," though, hardly amount to true solidarity.

Nevertheless, the gesture did have a number of short-term effects. It had the intended result of raising the profile of the situation and alleviating some of the acute repression against those working on behalf of victims. It also attracted significant international media interest, including from *Al Jazeera*, which embraced the corruption angle and explored it in depth with a documentary. Yet, as the film approached release, several of its key sources – people who had become my

26. Arthur Eremita, "Cambodian Propaganda: Playing the Victim to Get Away with Murder," *The Diplomat*, Oct. 31, 2023.

Photograph by Roman Koenig, from his series
*Glimpses of the Slums of Phnom Penh*, Cambodia, 2021–22.

friends – began receiving death threats and had to quickly exit the country. Shortly thereafter, I was advised to leave as well – just for a few days, till things settled down.

We left milk in the fridge and our cats with a friend. It was just a few days, after all. And once abroad, all I could think about was the team and partners I had left behind, those courageous folks still under constant surveillance and intimidation. I'd agitated for this fight and I longed to be back in it. This felt like the moment to leave mere gestures of solidarity behind, to assume for the first time something like a real risk on behalf of those I had now grown to love. Didn't I owe them at least that much? Wasn't this my chance, at last, to really make a difference? Wasn't this my true *imperative to engage*?

On the other hand, who was I fooling? I was and am a Western development professional and there were just a few months left on my contract – was I really supposed to risk my life and freedom for that?

Things never did settle down, and in time my friend's prediction was borne out.

When "*they* came" for me, it wasn't so dramatic as it sounds. Just a few well-placed quiet threats and whispers. In all likelihood, mere bluffs. But who can say? And, no, I didn't "just leave." Ultimately, my employers judged that they were "unable to gain full confidence in the safety of Jacob's return to Cambodia," graciously removing the final decision from my hands.[27]

In the end, all that is immaterial and the same result stands. When they came for me, *I* left and *they* remained.

So here I sit, typing away in a hip, third-wave coffee bar in Bangkok – far from the dust and grease of my beloved Lone Pine burritos, farther still from

27. Jack Brook, "Threats Force Anti-trafficking NGO Director Out of Cambodia," *Nikkei Asia*, June 24, 2023.

Photograph by Roman Koenig, from his series
*Glimpses of the Slums of Phnom Penh*, Cambodia, 2021–22.

the people I traveled across the world to serve.

Almost overnight and without any real merit or effort, I went from "expat program leader" to "expert advisor." Now I'm the sort of person who gets quoted in the *Economist* or *VICE World News* or the *New York Times* because I bring gritty field experience to a medium-sized global news item. I'm the guy who gets to do op-eds and podcasts and leverage my "contextual knowledge" and "subject-matter expertise" on panels and in workshops in fancy hotels. Misgivings and indiscretions notwithstanding, I still have a place in this industry of aid. My resistance to the system is merely incorporated into its perpetuation, and my own.

Yet, as my time in Cambodia wound to a close, the situation on the ground was not all grim. A few brave Cambodian human-rights defenders got temporary cover while I took heat for a bit. My friend the quippy local journalist was rightly honored with some prestigious awards that I pray raise the costs of his government "coming for him." Some forced-labor victims are free today as a result of my brave local team and our partners. Together, we materially increased the cost of doing a very bad business and are at the forefront of a global response. Some exploiters may now be a bit less brazen with their abuses.

My fear, though, is that this too will fade quickly into the thick, hazy Cambodian sun as a new crop of professionals arrive with their own imperatives to engage, seeing only what they want to see. Truly seeing a place is an endeavor that takes a lifetime – and there are few from my world willing to give one.

As for me, sitting here safe, upwardly mobile, and somewhat disillusioned, I am humbled for the millionth time by the distance between my ideals and my actions.

I'm still wearing cheap clothes probably made in sweatshops by the same slaves I crossed the globe to protect. I'm still, frequently, paying more attention to my damned phone with the cobalt battery mined by child laborers in the Congo than I am to my own precious, deliciously cooing little girl. I'm still happily cherishing the security of my stateside private property, my paycheck, my (now unfrozen) bank accounts that promise a life of undeserved comfort amid a suffering world.

My eyes are open. I see these things and I know them. I'm still searching for how to become something different.

I wonder what "becoming something different" might mean for someone like me, who fears stumbling blindly through an incoherent life. I think again about my friend who says, "When they come for you, you may go, but we remain."

I think of Kem Ley who was shot down and of those who continue to suffer for their unwillingness to remain silent in the face of grave oppression.[28]

I think of another man who once said, "For whoever would save his life will lose it, but whoever loses his life for my sake will find it," (Luke 9:24) and how the key to understanding the paradox is love.

Love cannot exist in philosophical abstractions or contractual arrangements. It cannot exist in powerful institutions or other macro forms of social organization. Rather, love is personal and particular. Love looks like longevity and commitment, and a willingness to sacrifice our desires for the good of another.

This radical act may cost us our comfort, our security, even our lives. Yet, once we begin to open our eyes in love, we cannot help but recognize that the freedom of sight far surpasses any alternative. ➤

28. Arthur Eremita, "The Collateral Damage of the Hun Manet Charm Offensive," *The Diplomat*, Feb. 7, 2024; Bryony Lau, "Cambodia: Environmental Activists Sentenced to 6 to 8 Years," Human Rights Watch, July 2, 2024; "Cambodia: Smear Campaign against Labor Group," Human Rights Watch, July 2, 2024.

Vahe Yeremyan, *Boat*, oil on canvas, 2020

# Yearning for Freedom

*Augustine of Hippo, Dorothee Soelle,*
*Oscar Romero, and the White Rose*

*Augustine (AD 354–430) was bishop of Hippo and
one of the Latin Fathers of the Church.*

Now the only genuine freedom is that possessed by those who are happy and cleave to the eternal law; I am talking about the sort of freedom that people have in mind when they think they are free because they have no human masters, or that people desire when they want to be set free by their masters. Then come parents, brothers and sisters, a spouse, children, neighbors, relatives, friends, and anyone who is bound to us by some need. Next is the city itself, which frequently takes the place of the parents, together with honors, praise, and what is called popular acclaim. And finally comes property, which includes anything over which the law gives us control and which we have a recognized right to sell or give away.

This is our freedom, when we are subject to the truth; and the truth is God himself, who frees us from death, that is, from the state of sin. For that truth, speaking as a human being to those who believe in him, says, "If you abide in my word, you are truly my disciples. And you shall know the truth, and the truth shall make you free." For the soul enjoys nothing with freedom unless it enjoys it securely.

Now no one is secure in enjoying goods that can be lost against his will. But no one can lose truth and wisdom against his will, for no one can be separated from the place where they are. What we called separation from truth and wisdom is really just a perverse will that loves inferior things, and no one wills something unwillingly. We can all enjoy it equally and in common; there is ample room, and it lacks for nothing. It welcomes all of its lovers without envy; it belongs to them all but is faithful to each.

Augustine, *On Free Choice of the Will*, trans. Thomas Williams (Hackett, 1993), 25, 57. Used by permission.

*Dorothee Soelle (1929–2003) was a German liberation theologian and author. She spoke out against the Vietnam War, the Cold War arms race, and injustices in the developing world.*

FOR ME THE WORD FREEDOM has become an increasingly important word. I think every generation has the right to redefine this word. And if it has the right, it also has the duty. After having worked long in the European and transatlantic peace movement, I believe that freedom, a deeper inner idea of freedom, will not be attained until we are free of bombs, free of poison gas, free of the arms industry, and free of this whole cancer that overruns our entire life, defines our cities, rules our research, and terrorizes our landscapes with its low-flying aircraft that cause schoolchildren to scream and cry at night because they are so disturbed.

Freedom, true freedom, has become for me an intense yearning for a freedom from the most dreadful scourge of humanity, war. . . .

One day people will speak about war and preparation for war as we speak today about slavery. Perhaps the day will come when people understand that we can live without nuclear slavery, without conventional slavery, without chemical slavery, and without all the forms of this slavery that claim our minds and use us for their madness – 51 percent of all scientists and engineers work for death within the First World. I believe that we define freedom correctly when our ideas grow with us and are not left behind, that is, when our own intellectual growth, our judgment, capacity for truth, and search for truth develop so that we have different ideas with more reality. Thus I would like most to pray: "Free me, O God, from the dreadful historical role of the middle class in rich countries. Let my thirst for liberation grow."

It has become clearer and clearer to me that freedom is always liberation. . . . Where the Spirit of God is, there is liberation: *liberación*, not only *libertas* but the process of liberation. The more of the Spirit of God we have, the more visible become the prisons in which we live, on which we build, and in which we let others go to ruin.

Dorothee Soelle, *On Earth as in Heaven: A Liberation Spirituality of Sharing*, trans. Marc Batko (Westminster John Knox, 1993). Used by permission.

Vahe Yeremyan, *Harbor*, oil on canvas, 2022.

*Oscar Romero (1917–80) was archbishop of San Salvador. On March 23, 1980, he was murdered as he delivered a sermon in which he asked Salvadoran soldiers to stop carrying out the government's repression and violations of basic human rights.*

THERE CAN BE NO FREEDOM as long as there is sin in the heart. What's the use of changing structures? What's the use of violence and armed force if the motivation is hatred and the purpose is to buttress those in power or else to overthrow them and then create new tyrannies? What we seek in Christ is true freedom, the freedom that transforms the heart, the freedom the risen Christ announces to us today, "Seek what is above" (Col. 3:1). Don't view earthly freedom and the oppression of this unjust system in El Salvador just by looking down from the rooftops. Look on high! That doesn't mean accepting the situation, because Christians also know how to struggle. Indeed, they know that their struggle is more forceful and valiant when it is inspired by this Christ who knew how to do more than turn the other cheek and let himself be nailed to a cross. Even submitting to crucifixion, he has redeemed the world and sung the definitive hymn of victory, the victory that cannot be used for other ends but benefits those who, like Christ, are seeking the true liberation of human beings.

This liberation is incomprehensible without the risen Christ, and it's what I want for you, dear sisters and brothers, especially those of you who have such great social awareness and refuse to tolerate the injustices in our country. It's wonderful that God has given you this keen sensibility, and if you have a political calling, then blessed be God! Cultivate it well, and be careful not to lose that vocation. Don't replace that social and political sensitivity with hatred, vengeance, and earthly violence. Lift your hearts on high, and consider the things that are above!

Oscar Romero, homily delivered on April 15, 1979, in *A Prophetic Bishop Speaks to His People: The Complete Homilies of Archbishop Oscar Arnulfo Romero*, 6 vols., trans. Joseph Owens (Convivium, 2016), 4:372–73. Used by permission.

Vahe Yeremyan, *Old Harbor*, oil on canvas, 2023.

*The White Rose, an undercover resistance movement of university students in Nazi Germany, printed and distributed leaflets to expose Nazi atrocities. The Gestapo arrested and executed them in 1943. Sophie Scholl was twenty-one; her brother Hans, twenty-four; Christoph Probst, twenty-three; Alexander Schmorell and Willi Graf, twenty-five.*

EVERYWHERE AND AT ALL TIMES demons have been lurking in the dark, waiting for the moment when man is weak; when of his own volition he leaves his place in the order of creation as founded for him by God in freedom; when he yields to the force of evil, separates himself from the powers of a higher order; and after voluntarily taking the first step, he is driven on to the next and the next at a furiously accelerating rate. Everywhere and at all times of greatest trial men have appeared, prophets and saints who cherished their freedom, who preached the one God and who with his help brought the people to a reversal of their downward course. Man is free, to be sure, but without the true God he is defenseless against the principle of evil. He is a like rudderless ship, at the mercy of the storm, an infant without his mother, a cloud dissolving into thin air.

I ask you, you as a Christian wrestling for the preservation of your greatest treasure, whether you hesitate, whether you incline toward intrigue, calculation, or procrastination in the hope that someone else will raise his arm in your defence? Has God not given you the strength, the will to fight? ⇒

From the Fourth Leaflet, trans. Arthur R. Schultz, *The White Rose: Munich, 1942–1943*, © 1983 by Inge Aicher-Scholl. Published by Wesleyan University Press. Used by permission.

Vahe Yeremyan, *Seashore*, oil on canvas, 2019.

# Editors' Picks

### American Mother

*By Colum McCann
and Diane Foley*
(Bloomsbury, 240 pages)

On August 19, 2014, the world was stunned when ISIS uploaded a video to YouTube showing the beheading of James Foley. James, a journalist who had been kidnapped in 2012 in Syria, was the first American killed by ISIS. *American Mother*, written by Irish novelist Colum McCann with Diane Foley, James's mother, gracefully broaches the unfathomable barbarism of James's death, his passionate career in journalism, US policies on war and hostage negotiation, and the unfillable absence after the loss of a child.

The first section, written in the third person, narrates Diane Foley's meeting with Alexanda Kotey, a British national who had joined ISIS and pled guilty for his role in kidnapping, torturing, and killing four people, including James. The one thing Diane trusts throughout this harrowing meeting – and before, while navigating US policies and officials during James's imprisonment and after his death – is her faith that God will provide her the strength, courage, and grace to defend the dignity of both her son and his captors.

In the next section, the book is narrated by Diane in the first person, beginning with a retelling of the day she learned her son had been killed and the subsequent cloud of grief. She and McCann write vividly about the profound absence and sense of helplessness that occurred after James's death. Subsequent sections of the book detail James's life and his dedication to telling the stories of people involved in or otherwise impacted by conflict. While *American Mother* is about James's death, it is also about the faith that sustained Diane to wake up each morning, to advocate for hostages and their families, and to face the men who murdered her son. While Diane could not anticipate her son's death, she seems uniquely positioned to receive even this tragedy as an opportunity to seek the grace of God.

The book is particularly strong in assessing the role of the US government in hostage negotiation. Many European countries can and do negotiate for the release of their citizens held abroad. The United Kingdom and the United States, however, generally do not. All non-British and non-Americans held by ISIS were released, while the British and American hostages were killed. Though neither McCann nor Diane are experts in foreign policy, they write persuasively in support of revisiting the policies that led to James's death.

Despite its painful and harrowing subject material, *American Mother* is a book of hope for America, an America full of strangers seeking to console a family bearing unimaginable loss, an America that can prioritize the lives of its citizens. McCann and Foley write with grace and conviction about the need for moral courage in the bleakest moments of life. It is only through the cultivation of such courage that James was able to report on conflict in Syria and that Diane Foley was able to do the work she has since in trying to make sense of her son's death. However dark life may be, relying on faith to find courage and grace can provide a means for preserving the memory of those lost.
　　　　　　　　　　　—*Sharla Moody*

### I Cheerfully Refuse
A Novel

**By Leif Enger**
*(Grove Atlantic,
497 pages)*

For an author who has lived in Minnesota his entire life, Leif Enger takes a keen interest in stories of exile. He made a splash with his debut novel, *Peace Like a River* (2001), which sold over one million copies. The story follows a miracle-working janitor and two of his young children (one beset with asthma) fleeing the law and pursuing his oldest son. His next novel, *So Brave, Young, and Handsome* (2008), traces the journey of Monte Becket, whose desire for absolution leads him away from home in the hopes he can return a new man. And *Virgil Wander* (2018) tells the story of a man exiled from his own mind after experiencing a car crash and witnessing the return of a prodigal. All these novels circle around themes of exile, guilt, journeying, and the desire and difficulty of being at home. Enger's most recent novel, *I Cheerfully Refuse* (2024), tells the same tale, with a post-apocalyptic twist.

Set in a not-too-distant future, with a geopolitical context assumed and alluded to but never explained, the book's post-apocalyptic world is eerily believable. "Astronauts" (one thinks of Elon Musk) live far away from ordinary people who are subject to the vagaries of a collapsed society following a plague. Society has regressed to a sort of Wild West libertarianism, which admittedly has its charms. But dark omens lurk: old bodies once preserved in the cool water of Lake Superior float to the surface due to the rising temperatures of climate change. The Willow drug appears, "a rising star on the market of despair," claiming lives to suicide.

When his contented life with his charming bookselling wife, Lark, is disturbed by an act of inexplicable violence, the protagonist, Rainy, finds himself adrift on Lake Superior, running from the barbaric and mysterious Werryck. In many ways, reading this book felt like living through the last few years: unlikely and distressing things kept happening in confusing succession, which seem to be, as Shakespeare would put it, "full of sound and fury, signifying nothing." The book is darker than Enger's previous novels, the plot less clear and cohesive, the resolution less clean. And yet in this meandering moral messiness there is something valuable. While Rainy does not possess a refined or intellectual moral compass, he is guided through this listless world by an indomitable impulse to protect the vulnerable from the bullies. This humane habit preserves him from despair, providing something of a model for what it might look like to live well in the morally ambiguous times in which we find ourselves; what the day calls for are not pristine moral philosophers but persons who do not abandon their own or others' humanity.

Readers will find a murkier world than they may be used to in Enger's novels, but this only matches the troubled world in which we find ourselves. And, like Rainy, they may also learn to cheerfully refuse to resign themselves to the despair of the contemporary world.

*—Joy Marie Clarkson*

## Fully Alive
### Tending to the Soul in Turbulent Times

*By Elizabeth Oldfield*
*(Brazos, 272 pages)*

It is a gift to be alive, and a fragmenting, anxious world can either numb this knowing or rouse it. As I think of the uncertain future my young daughter will face, I want her to step into her aliveness, to gather courage and live from a deep center, and like a tree with roots sunk deep into the ground, to stay standing when the storms come. I want this for myself too.

*Fully Alive* is the book I need right now. Its title is from a quotation attributed to Saint Irenaeus: "The glory of God is a human being fully alive." We are to be rooted in our humanity as well as to hope in heaven, and Elizabeth Oldfield invites us – secular and religious alike – to look with her through the lens of the Christian tradition at the "ancient technologies" that might help us find steadiness and "spiritual core strength." Her quest is structured, unexpectedly, around the seven deadly sins. "Fully aliveness, for me, is summed up in connection, and my definition of sin is everything working against that." She unearths sins as modes of disconnection and explores their opposites – qualities to work toward rather than away from: wrath (from polarization to peacemaking), envy (from status anxicty to belovedness), pride (from individualism to community), and so on.

Oldfield offers personal stories, wisdom, and practices that she and generations before her have found helpful: prayer, liturgy, and community. These also act as guardrails for her attention. What we pay attention to is what we will become, and Oldfield wants to become someone who is "growing outwards and upwards into love." But our attention is fast becoming a commodity, pulling us outward, leaving the inner landscape neglected. *Fully Alive* tends that landscape.

Until the final chapter, Oldfield uses "[God]" throughout, recognizing that people will bring their own ideas into the space between the brackets. She is not setting out to offer an argument for Christianity, but rather "signposts and support to become the kind of human that I think this world might need." One of those needs is for people who can depolarize the world. My experience in community work and local politics is that divisions often fade when we get up close, and I wonder if these polarizing times are less about difference itself (essential for life to thrive) and more about the decline in opportunities to encounter people "not like me." Oldfield shares her experiences of church and the "micro community" her family lives in, structures that offer opportunities to encounter love and resist the tides that threaten to "pull us away from each other." She also explores this theme in her podcast, *The Sacred*.

Oldfield is vulnerable as she grapples with questions of how to live (readers may laugh, blush, disagree, empathize), and her relatability brings secular and sacred into closer alignment. *Fully Alive* is a wise and luminous call to wholeness, to community – to stand in the turbulence between the world as it is and as it could be and trust that we were made for such times as these.

*—Elizabeth Wainwright*

# Slaves to One Another

T HE LETTERS OF THE APOSTLE PAUL contain a clarion call to freedom that has rung down the centuries: "For freedom Christ has set us free. Stand firm, therefore, and do not submit again to a yoke of slavery" (Gal. 5:1). Paul's theology has given weight to an age-old yearning of the human spirit to be free to think, choose, and act. It has also inspired social and political movements that seek freedom from human domination and coercion in its various forms. Indeed, freedom has become the watchword of Western modernity, but with a radically individualized tone: autonomy, independence, and choice have become unquestionable virtues for the "buffered" self that is wary of obligations and prefers to determine which responsibilities to adopt, or to discard, in the quest for self-fulfillment. Freedom as self-determination seems, on the surface, a natural extension of the theology of Paul.

Not so fast! As soon as he issues his call to freedom, Paul adds a crucial dialectic. "You were called to freedom, brothers and sisters; only do not use your freedom as an opportunity for self-indulgence [literally: the flesh], but through love become slaves to one another" (Gal. 5:13). Paul knows he is using paradox: employ your freedom for slavery! But this is not a rhetorical trick; these are two sides of the same coin. As he remarks in Romans, "While we were living in the flesh, our sinful passions, aroused by the law, were at work in our members to bear fruit for death. But now we are discharged from the law, dead to that which held us captive, so that we are slaves not under the old written code, but in the new life of the Spirit" (Rom. 7:5–6). Released from captivity in order to be slaves, but slaves of one kind, and not of another. In Romans as in Galatians, "slavery" in the new life of the Spirit takes the form of love: "Owe no one anything, except to love one another. For the one who loves another has fulfilled the law" (Rom. 13:8). The freedom Paul proclaims is not individual autonomy or independence, but the freedom that takes place within the mutual commitments of love. What does he mean?

Paul understands the world not as an empty space in which individuals carve out their private sphere of freedom, but as a terrain already populated by competing powers greater than human actors, who only imagine that they are free. As far as Paul is concerned, our search for an individuated, atomized autonomy is itself an enslaving delusion, because we are, and are meant to be, free only as we are formed by relationships with God and with others. God is powerfully active in the world, in creation and re-creation, and the basic stance of human recognition of God is an act of trust that is at the same time a form of submission ("the obedience of faith," Rom. 1:5). To recognize God's saving act in Jesus Christ is to say, "Jesus is Lord" (Greek, *kyrios*, which means master; 1 Cor. 12:3). The fulfillment of human potential will come about not through the imagined freedom of an independent self, but through submission to the resurrection power of Jesus, when every knee will bend and every tongue confess that Jesus Christ is Lord (Phil. 2:11). Only then will "creation be freed from its bondage to decay" (Rom. 8:21). Only then will humans reach their ultimate fulfillment and will Christ "transform the body of our humiliation so that it may be conformed to the body of his glory, by the power that also enables him to make all things subject to himself" (Phil. 3:21). The true freedom from all that restricts human completeness, including sickness, suffering, and death, is possible only because the "Lord" (*kyrios*) Jesus is more powerful than all the forces that constrain and constrict our flourishing.

---

*John M. G. Barclay is a British biblical scholar and historian of early Christianity. He is the current Lightfoot Professor of Divinity at Durham University in Durham, England, with a focus on the New Testament.*

Rembrandt, *Saint Paul in Prison*, oil on canvas, 1627.

Those forces are bigger than we imagine them to be in our little privatized worlds. They are the social and cultural forces that shape our worldviews and constrain our imaginations; they are the political forces that (now with even greater success) watch and control our movements. And, most importantly, they are the macrostructures of human existence. They are our appalling propensity to cruelty, indifference, prejudice, folly, and selfishness, which Paul labels simply "sin." And beyond that, they are our physical fragility and mortality that Paul calls "decay" and "death." He pictures the world as a cosmic battlefield, in which we are entangled whether we recognize it or not. What God is doing in Jesus is a loving act of liberation from occupying powers. Jesus, whose resurrection has blasted a way through death, is subduing all that spoils and inhibits our potential to flourish (1 Cor. 15:20–28). We will find freedom not in our own puny strength, but by enlistment into the victorious progress of "the Lord." That march to freedom, confident in the security of God's love, already frees us from the self-concern and insecurities that lie at the root of human "sin." "Where the Spirit of the Lord is, there is freedom" (2 Cor. 3:17).

Given that big picture, what does it mean to be "free" but "slaves" within the ordinary run of human life? The theme of freedom runs through several of Paul's letters, but nowhere more powerfully than in his letter to the Galatians. Here he resists what he calls the "compulsion" of those who seek to impose on Christian believers a particular set of religious and cultural practices, as if that were the only way to belong to Christ. The presenting issue is the demand by competing missionaries that male believers get circumcised, according to the Jewish law, thus restricting "the freedom that we have in Christ Jesus" (Gal. 2:4; 6:12). What Paul opposes here is not "Judaism" as such, but the attempt to constrain Christian identity within the boundaries of *one* socio-cultural tradition. This fundamentally contradicts the barrier-crossing grace of God in Christ, which is "free" in its disregard of preexisting human conditions and acts without regard to differences of ethnicity, status, or gender (Gal. 3:28). What this grace brings about is a freedom to reconsider and reconfigure all the social and cultural values that we have inherited and in which we were raised, with a radical freshness that Paul attributes to "new creation" (Gal. 6:15). And the purpose of this freedom is to create the possibility of new, boundary-breaking communities that cross the lines of prejudice, discrimination, and fear, and provide new forms of belonging to one another in love: "for in Christ Jesus neither circumcision nor uncircumcision counts for anything; the only thing that counts is faith [or trust] working through love" (Gal. 5:6).

Paul propounds the paradox of freedom *and slavery* at the human level because the "slavery" he has in mind is, as we have seen, the mutual slavery of love: "Do not use your freedom as an opportunity for self-indulgence, but through love become slaves to one another." He understands (and we too often forget) that humans are constituted by relationships, not by self-definition, and his vision for human flourishing is not that of isolated individuals who chart their own paths through life with as few commitments as possible, but the self-in-relation, the people who reach their human potential through life *with* others, in the mutual self-giving of love. All of Paul's letters

A cast copper-alloy Roman tumbler lock slide key with chain, AD 43–410.

drive toward the formation of cross-cultural and cross-status communities whose members work out together how best to practice their commitment to Christ. As he makes clear in his famous image of the body of Christ, all the members have something to contribute to others and something that they need from others; no one is self-sufficient and capable of flourishing alone (1 Cor. 12:12–26). What holds this community together is what Paul calls *koinōnia* (solidarity or partnership) – solidarity with Christ (experienced in the Lord's Supper) and partnership with one another. And the glue in that solidarity is love – love received from Christ, who gave himself "for me" (Gal. 2:19–20) and "for you" (1 Cor. 11:24), and love shared with one another (1 Cor. 13).

The freedom to love is the freedom to receive, offer, and share ties of belonging, and therefore ties of obligation. Paul understands what has happened in the life, death, and resurrection of Christ as the ultimate and definitive act of divine love (Rom. 5:6–11), a love that comes alongside us and inhabits our condition in order to break the shackles of all that constrains our fulfillment, freeing us to find our completion in trust and allegiance to Christ. That love is now "poured into our hearts by the Holy Spirit that has been given us" (Rom. 5:5). Being love, it is expressed in bonds of commitment, trust, loyalty, and patience toward others, and the same is expected of them. Love does not give the self away, but it gives the self *into* solidarity with others, fulfilling our deepest needs and longings not in splendid isolation, which is not so splendid after all, but in co-flourishing with others. As in Luther's brilliant pamphlet *The Freedom of a Christian* (still essential reading for any thoughtful Christian), it is because we are free from self-concern, secured by the love of God, that we are able to be slaves of others (1 Cor. 9:19). The love that we share, which is the expression and extension of the love of God, is also a kind of love-return to God – we express love, trust, and gratitude to God *in* love of one another – so that

---

*Paul considered everyone, slave or free, to have the immeasurable worth of being loved by Christ, who died for all.*

---

the freedom that we enjoy in love ties us both to one another and to God. How can we be free to be our best selves? Not in cutting (or diminishing) our ties to others, but in freedom from the self-centeredness that we falsely worship as freedom, and thus in immersing ourselves into the bonds (and hazards) of love, confident that, whatever our own failures in such an endeavor, it is the path that will ultimately be vindicated and completed in God's loving consummation of ourselves and of all things in Christ.

BUT WHAT DID ALL THIS mean for those who were literally enslaved? Slavery was endemic to the social and economic world in which Paul lived – as fundamental and near unquestionable as our modern notion of private property. Paul encountered many

A length of copper-alloy chain dating back to the Roman Empire.

a slave within and outside his churches, most famously Onesimus, who probably asked him to make an appeal to his owner, Philemon, and who became a Christian in the process (see the little gem, Paul's letter to Philemon). Paul considered everyone, slave or free, to have the immeasurable worth of being loved by Christ, who died for all (2 Cor. 5:14–15). For him, slaves were not mere "things" (the property of their owners); it was possible to see them in an entirely different way (no longer regarded "from a human point of view," 2 Cor. 5:16). Those who belonged to Christ (like the new Onesimus) were "a new creation" (2 Cor. 5:17), beneficiaries of the liberating action of Christ, and with an identity and worth the same as any free man or woman (Gal. 3:28; 1 Cor. 12:13). Indeed, since Christ had effected the deepest and most meaningful realignment of power in the universe, what ultimately mattered more than any form of human belonging was the question of who belonged to Christ. "You have been bought with a price," says Paul to all the believers in Corinth (1 Cor. 6:20; 7:23). Through his death and resurrection, Christ has bought them out of those destructive forms of enslavement that thwart human flourishing and placed them into a new form of commitment ("enslavement") where they can become all they were meant to be. Paul can thus say, "Whoever was called in the Lord as a slave is a freed person belonging to the Lord, just as whoever was free when called is a slave of Christ" (1 Cor. 7:22). Freed persons (slaves manumitted by their owners) still had continuing obligations to the Lord. No one in this picture is free in our imagined terms of individualized autonomy, because in Paul's view, no such state is possible. Everyone is in one kind of slavery (to sin and death) or another (to righteousness and life, Rom. 6:15–23). The only question is who you call "Lord." The slaves in Paul's picture have the dignity of being freed persons of the only Lord who has their ultimate welfare fully at heart and fully in his capacity to grant.

But what of their human welfare in the conditions of the here-and-now? Slavery could be immensely cruel: slave families could be split up when individual members were sold, and slaves could be subject to dehumanizing treatment, including sexual abuse. Most slaves wished to be manumitted, so long as they had a chance to make a living thereafter; and owners were often willing to grant this, so long as someone could pay for it, and so long as it served to encourage compliant behavior among other slaves. What does Paul ask for? In the case of Onesimus, whom his owner considered "useless" and may have threatened to sell (Philem. 11), Paul asks that he be welcomed back "forever" (i.e., not sold out of the household), "no longer as a slave, but as more than a slave, a beloved brother" (Philem. 15–16). This is not a clear request for manumission, but it does expect a qualitative difference in the everyday treatment of Onesimus, in the household of Philemon and in the wider Christian community that meets there (Philem. 1–3). Paul here resets the relationship between Onesimus and Philemon at such a fundamental level that manumission is now far more likely to be an eventual outcome. Elsewhere, Paul encourages slaves to make use of their freedom if it is offered (the best translation of 1 Cor. 7:21, as most scholars now agree), and considers freedom rather than slavery a better condition in which to serve Christ (1 Cor. 7:23: "you were bought with a price; do not become slaves of human masters").

Cast copper-alloy keys dating back to the early Roman Empire.

Even if Paul had requested Onesimus's manumission (which would have required a lot of face-to-face discussion), that would not have been a call for the abolition of slavery: manumission was a mechanism *within* ancient slavery, not, as we might think, a means to its dissolution. We must face squarely the fact that Paul did *not* call for the abolition of slavery as we, with hindsight, might have hoped and expected. One could offer pragmatic explanations (it was economically inconceivable, or would have sounded too radical), but the basic explanation is probably this: Paul did not see, as we now do, that the ownership of a human being is a basic injustice. The difference is due to a fundamental shift in modern Western thought regarding human rights, a shift that we can properly claim as a legitimate *extension* of Paul's theology, but not one he envisaged himself. If we were to develop Paul's own terms, the problem of slavery to a human owner is not that it denies autonomy (which is neither possible nor a means to human flourishing) but that it restricts or denies the capacity to serve God and others in love. Human beings owned are human beings lawfully constrained in their capacity to decide, choose, and act; they are therefore unable freely (and thus fully) to commit themselves to others, or to God. They are also liable to receive treatment that is contrary to love, but that cannot be effectively challenged because of the owners' legal rights over their "property." Paul did not see that as clearly as we now do, and unfortunately, his letters have been used to defend recent forms of slavery as much as to criticize it. At this point we would have to take a stance explicitly both *with* and *beyond* Paul: with him in urging the freedom that brings human fulfillment without the false expectation of autonomy, but beyond him in seeing slavery in itself as a fundamental obstacle to that possibility.

In any case, it is clear that freedom for Paul meant more than something "spiritual" or

"inner," as many modern forms of Christianity make out. Freedom is about the God-given release from all that inhibits and undermines our human potential as creatures of God, and thus from the multiple layers of constraint under which we operate, from coercive control to cultural prejudice, from obsessive behavior to death itself, and all the various forms of unfreedom in between. "For freedom Christ has set us free" at every level of our being. But ironically (or so it might seem to the modern mind), our freedom is acquired and enjoyed not through self-determination, but through our alignment to the liberating power of another, Christ, and through our immersion in the self-sharing practices of love that bind us to one another in commitment and community. Our freedom to love is the way we resonate with the transcendent love that comes to meet us in Christ. That divine love calls us to sing the melody of reciprocal, committed, self-giving love, a melody that foretells the ultimate liberation of the universe. Because of that deep resonance with eternal truth, this song of freedom-in-love turns out to be greater than any of the other songs of liberation passed down through history. It is sung, incompletely but powerfully, in countless lives throughout the world today. "Do you hear the people sing?" (*Les Misérables*). ➤

# Taking Lifelong Vows

*Poverty, chastity, and obedience*
*might sound confining. They can bring*
*a different kind of liberation.*

**DORI MOODY**

RAISED IN A LOVING FAMILY, I knew of God from my first breath. I was part of the third generation to be born in the Bruderhof, a Christian communal movement that began in the 1920s. To me, being a Bruderhof child meant growing up in a happy world, one rich in both family and community.

I loved the group mealtimes with over two hundred people in a large dining hall. It was fun to eat and sing together. Sometimes the older people did skits or performances. Other times children gave recitals. As a community, we had picnics, watched movies, went on hikes, and held church services together. The school allowed for hours of outdoor

C. M. Dudash, *Rose Shadow Study*, oil on linen, 2003.

play – bare feet permitted until the first snowflakes fell; opportunities to ride horses, swim, ski, skate, and toboggan – not to mention the many indoor activities: hours in the pottery studio messing about with clay, or crafting homemade marshmallows in the school kitchen. Wonderful teachers introduced me to literature and art. I loved the library, and I lived in the stories I read.

But a glorious childhood did not prevent me from becoming an egocentric teenager. Perhaps growing up with God, good examples, and the safe boundaries of a close-knit church saved me from some mistakes, but these did not save me from selfishness. I was aware that the sacrifices adults who lived in community made were real: they gave up their money and time, and they devoted all hours of the day to each other and God. I was not interested in that. After a turbulent junior year, I dropped out of high school, kissed goodbye the supportive efforts of my parents, and flew to a smaller Bruderhof in Germany.

Far from home, I cheerfully set about doing exactly as I wished. I found friends who, like me, pushed away the big decisions, choosing instead the momentary dissipation of youth. It was easy for me to turn on the loving people who raised me, and mock people who did not measure up to my idea of "normal." I laughed at the old-world costume Bruderhof members wore, and I disparaged their morals as prudish piety. Despite attending church services and communal meals, I closed my ears to Christianity. How simple it was to oversleep, get away with minimal work, and live purposelessly, even on a Bruderhof community. But in my freedom from limits and obligations, I became desperately unhappy.

Secretly I envied the joy of my parents and others members outside my clique. It irritated me that they could be so fulfilled in what I saw as their narrow lives. I pined for similar joy, but what I really wanted was for God to make me happy with no effort on my part. Guilt gave me a stomachache. I did not sleep well, and I wagered with God at night. I promised him things in exchange for sleep, and then took back the promises in daylight.

One midnight, the dam broke. Desperate for peace, I arranged an appointment with my pastor and his wife. When the dreaded time came in the morning, my face glowed with shame as I poured out the lies and deceptions that had churned my guts, keeping me wide-eyed in the dark of night. Smiling faces, kind eyes, reassurance met my humiliation. The pastor offered not judgment, but hopeful words. His wife simply offered understanding: "You must have been so unhappy." Their words restored my shattered confidence.

I spoke out my sins initially for relief from torment. But the act of confession gave birth to contrition. I felt sorry for how I had hurt God, my parents, my peers. Remorse gave me a new outlook. I understood for the first time that God required something of me, and, grateful to be released from the weight of guilt, I wished only to serve the God who truly frees.

ALAS, IN AN EARNEST DESIRE to be perfect for God, I tumbled from repentance not to peace, but frustration and despair. As the saying goes, the devil really was in the details.

Prioritizing perfection unleashed two new fiends. Devil One pointed out other people's failings. Suddenly those around me did not measure up to my ideals. In the past my friends' and coworkers' shortcomings had not bothered me at all. Now I had no patience for their weaknesses.

When I was not annoyed at others, Devil Two kept me perpetually afraid of people's opinions. I followed Christ's commandments not out of love, but because I wanted to be seen as correct. I feared the reaction of those around me more than the quiet voice of God inside me. Fear, not love, drove me to serve.

*Dori Moody is a Bruderhof member and an editor at* Plough. *She and her husband and children live at Danthonia, a Bruderhof community in New South Wales, Australia.*

Joy left me. I made radical changes in my life – avoiding the music and literature I loved, abandoning pursuits such as sports and social gatherings, and resolving each day not to waste a moment on myself. At every turn, I set about sacrificing myself for God and others. In a sense, these years were probably the most upright of my life – and the most miserable. How well I understood Martin Luther's complaint that "if one were to confess his sins in a timely manner, he would have to carry a confessor in his pocket!" I could not escape relentless temptations, and I felt ill-used by a God who wielded a mighty refining tool.

How strenuous to be good! At least living a life of evil and selfish pursuits had been fun (at the time), and confessing my sins had been difficult but straightforward. Three years later, I faced something even more confounding: how to overcome myself. I prayed for deliverance.

Little by little, grace penetrated my misery. The realization that God did not want my effort was an epiphany of grace. All the human determination, so earnest, so futile, faded away. Miraculously,

personal striving was replaced by a dizzying upward release, away from myself. In almost giddy gratitude, my searching and questioning merged into one simple response: How could I truly serve Jesus?

Three years from my gut-churning midnight encounter with God, I requested membership into the Bruderhof. Like any vocation to join a religious life, this was a deeply personal decision. It is not possible to be born into Bruderhof membership, just as it is not possible to be born into a convent or monastery. Children like me might be raised in the Bruderhof, but without a personal encounter with God, lifelong vows cannot be taken. Knowing that my parents and grandparents had made the very same commitment years before me did not make my decision a foregone conclusion, but, if anything, complicated it. Nonetheless, I discerned this calling for myself as well.

So it was that on January 14, 1995, I stood before a large congregation and proclaimed the ancient poetry of the Nicene Creed, affirming that I believed. Then, with joyful intention, I entered the pool and knelt. The waters rushed over my head three times and I rose, reborn. I became a sister. When I stepped out of the baptismal waters, dripping and joyful, I felt not that I had arrived, but that I must travel. A new life in Christ beckoned. I didn't want to be a solitary traveler, but part of a band – a troop of believers that spanned the centuries. I desired the camaraderie, accountability, and inspiration others could give. As Augustine of Hippo wrote in the fifth century, "He who does not have the church as his mother does not have God as his father." The church I sought was like a mother – a ferocious protector, a provider, a holy and beautiful expression of the Holy Spirit.

When I made a lifetime commitment to the Bruderhof I joined a community of families and singles who had also surrendered everything to serve Jesus and each other. Vows of faithfulness to

C. M. Dudash, *Red Daisies*, oil on linen, 2003.

my brothers and sisters linked me to the mother church that went back to the time of creation.

CONVERSION HAS BROUGHT ME life in threes. For every sinner, there is the old life, the new life, and the life to come. For every convert there is the Father, the Son, and the Holy Spirit. But for those who, like me, have made vows of lifetime faithfulness in a religious community, there are also the gospel counsels of poverty, chastity, and obedience.

These are not the easiest virtues to live by. Initially, they appear narrow and restrictive – how much of myself must be stripped away? What must I renounce in this world for the sake of the world to come? But this is not the only way to look at them. Daily life is a better measure of fulfillment, for I am happy, and yes, after almost thirty years of communal living, still a bit giddy.

Poverty is the easiest. Growing up the way I did helped. Even as a child, I saw what people did with their money, and I observed that stockpiling it did not produce happiness. The love of money often brought out weakness, while those who shared were like hardwood, resilient. I also knew that private property and the urge to hoard or collect earthly things was at best a distraction, at worst idolatry. Since I owned nothing before my commitment, a much larger consideration was the decision to lay down the possibility of future earnings. Now I am relieved to be free of personal ownership, to live a life of sharing.

Chastity is harder. Like many others, this did not come naturally to me, and I squirmed under chastity's great bright light. But repentance humbled my heart to appreciate the dangers it warned off. Sexual purity prior to marriage and fidelity within it hinge on my readiness to not grudgingly but wholeheartedly pledge agape as superior to all other forms of love. My love for Jesus must be deeper than my love for any human being.

Obedience is the hardest of all. Like every Christian, I wish to follow the Holy Spirit, but often conveniently confuse the third person of the Trinity with my own ideas. I seldom if ever feel a direct call from God that clearly tells me anything. Fortunately, repentance has tempered my mind. Over the years, I have developed a healthy doubt about my own wisdom, and a desire to listen to other church members. I've learned that the voice of the Holy Spirit speaks most certainly through other people. Occasionally my

---

**Years ago, the vertigo that accompanied my conversion disoriented me enough to see beyond the narrow definitions that poverty, chastity, and obedience sometimes hold.**

---

ideas match my coworkers', but sometimes my wishes are selfish, or they miss the bigger picture. No matter how inconvenient obedience is then, it protects me in my faith. George MacDonald wisely wrote, "What in the heart we call faith, in the will we call obedience." With humility, I've learned to receive clarity of direction through brothers and sisters who are also modeling respect and forbearance.

There are times of frustration with myself and perhaps equal times of disappointment with others, but in the end, life in church community does not depend on perfect human beings. Years ago, the vertigo that accompanied my conversion disoriented me enough to see beyond the narrow definitions that poverty, chastity, and obedience sometimes hold. These three gospel counsels remind me of the interconnecting nimbus of vines that halos the ringed or Celtic cross, with Jesus at the center. And this is our calling, to live a life close to the cross. ⇒

JOONAS SILDRE

# BETWEEN
# TWO
# SOUNDS

## ARVO PÄRT'S
## JOURNEY TO HIS
## MUSICAL LANGUAGE

TRANSLATED BY ADAM CULLEN

BUT WHAT IS THE RIGHT WAY? AND HOW TO FIND THE MEANS TO EMBARK UPON IT?

BY PLACING THE CHAOS OF HIS OWN MODERNIST COMPOSITION AND BACH'S
CALM AND ORDER SIDE BY SIDE, ARVO CREATES COLLAGES.

SO, YOU DON'T WORK IN RADIO ANYMORE? HOW'S YOUR HEALTH?

IT'S FINE. I'VE QUALIFIED FOR DISABILITY STATUS.

I'M TINKERING WITH A SYMPHONIC PIECE. IT TURNS THE PAGE ON EVERYTHING THAT'S COME BEFORE, IN A SENSE ...

I HOPE YOU'RE BEING CAREFUL. I'M GOING TO HAVE TO CUT THAT PART ABOUT RELIGION FROM THE PROGRAM SO IT DOESN'T SEEM LIKE YOU'VE COMPLETELY TURNED YOUR BACK ON THE OFFICIAL IDEOLOGY.

ESTONIA CONCERT HALL. NEEME JÄRVI IS CONDUCTING THE PREMIERE OF ARVO PÄRT'S "CREDO."

SHOULD WE PRACTICE IT ONCE MORE?

NO, THAT'S ENOUGH. SEE YOU TONIGHT.

IT'S BEING DONE BEHIND THE REGIME'S BACK AS, DUE TO A STRING OF COINCIDENCES, THE PIECE SLIPPED PAST EVERYONE WHO SHOULD HAVE IMMEDIATELY BLOCKED ITS PATH TO THE CONCERT HALL.

THE COMPOSERS' UNION LEADERSHIP IS AWAY AT A CONGRESS IN MOSCOW — WHEN THE CAT'S AWAY, THE MICE WILL PLAY ...

"CREDO" ...

IS THIS SOME RELIGIOUS THING?

"CREDO" IS A SUMMARY OF MY COLLAGE TECHNIQUE.

THE TRANSPLANTATION TECHNIQUE HAS REACHED ITS ULTIMATE LIMIT.

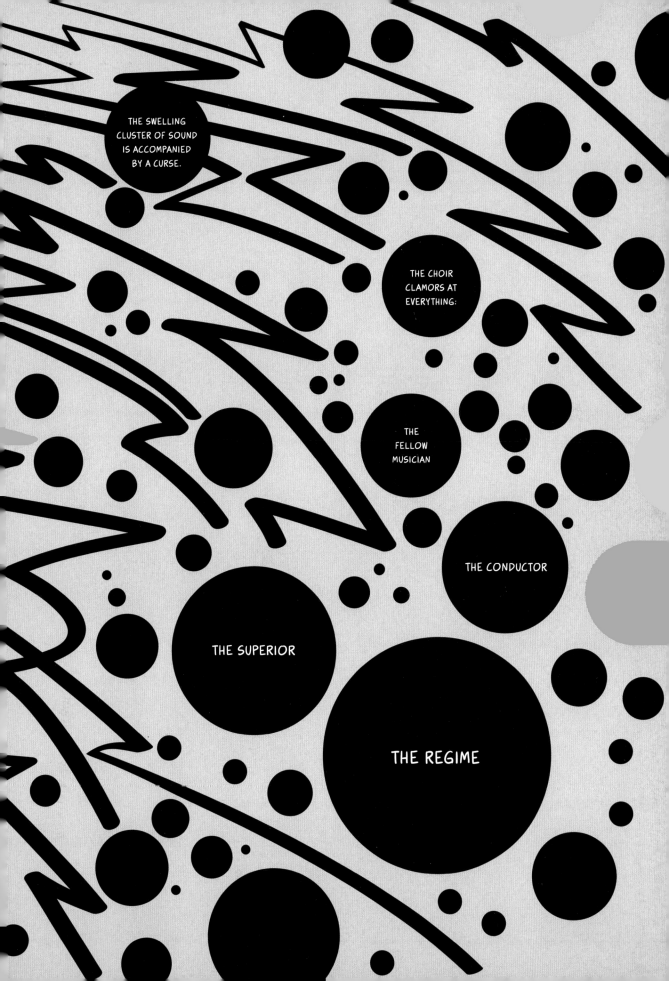

AT THE ULTIMATE LIMITS OF THE CLAMOR, BACH'S C MAJOR PRELUDE CUTS IN.

BUT I SAY

UNTO YOU

THAT YE RESIST

NO EVIL

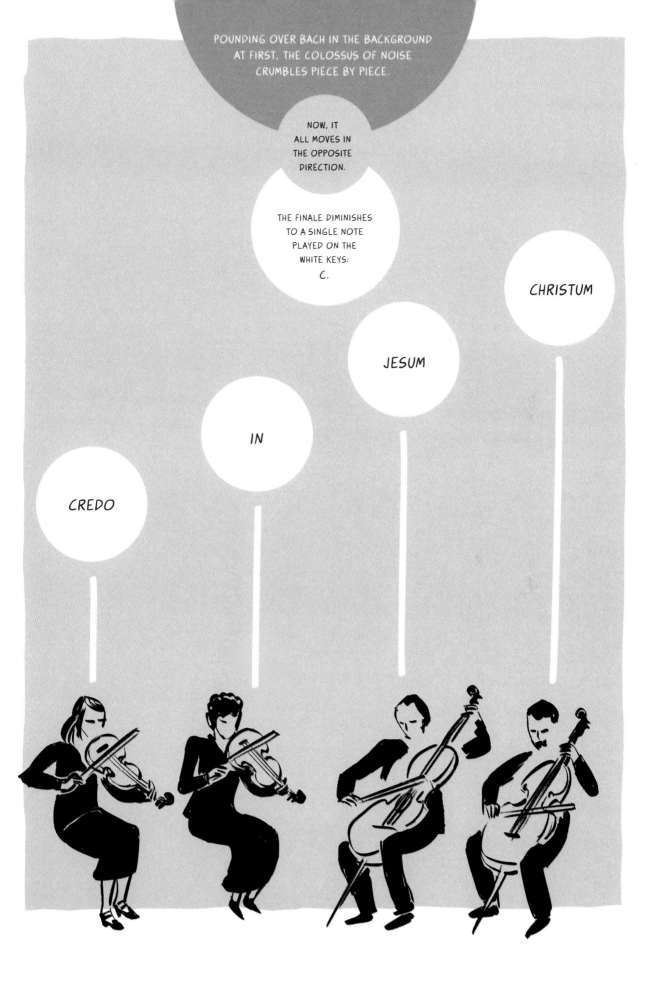

THE TALLINN-MOSCOW TRAIN, A FEW WEEKS AFTER THE PREMIERE OF "CREDO." A COMPOSERS' UNION DELEGATION IS EN ROUTE TO A CONGRESS.

COMRADE
PÄRT ...

"MISSA
CREDO"

CREDO IN UNUM
DEUM, PATREM
OMNIPOTENTEM
FACTOREM

A
CATHOLIC
MASS?

WE'RE ON
TO YOU.

PARTY FUNCTIONARIES APPEAR TO HAVE REALIZED THAT
SOMETHING ... UNSUITABLE ... SLIPPED THROUGH. YET
THEY DON'T SEEM TO BE ENTIRELY SURE JUST YET WHAT
EXACTLY THIS SOMETHING IS.

A FEW MONTHS LATER, ARVO IS CALLED IN FOR ANOTHER MEETING WITH OLAF UTT, SECRETARY OF CULTURE OF THE CENTRAL COMMITTEE OF THE COMMUNIST PARTY.

"CREDO IN JESUM CHRISTUM"?

WHAT ARE THE POLITICAL CONSIDERATIONS OF THIS WORK?

THE PIECE HAS NOTHING TO DO WITH POLITICS!

ITS MUSIC AND TEXT MERELY EXPRESS MY PERSONAL STANDPOINT.

YOU KNOW, I'M UNDER PRESSURE.

I GOT A VERY STERN CALL FROM MOSCOW ABOUT THIS "CREDO" AND IN GENERAL ... IT LOOKS VERY BAD FROM OVER THERE.

YOU'RE A DIFFICULT CASE ... EVERYTHING IN COMPOSERS' UNION MEMBERS' ANNUAL PLANS MUST BE DETAILED DOWN TO A T, BUT YOU ALWAYS WRITE SOMETHING OBSCURE ...

"TIME WILL TELL."

"WE SHALL SEE."

WE FEEL YOU'RE NOT FULLY PARTICIPATING IN SOVIET LIFE.

SEVERAL OF YOUR COLLEAGUES COULD SERVE AS ROLE MODELS IN TERMS OF ATTITUDE AND CREATIVE DIRECTION ...

BACH IS MY ROLE MODEL. IF I COULD ONLY ONE DAY SAY THAT EVERY NOTE I WRITE IS IN HONOR OF GOD!

THIS "CREDO" ...

WE'RE BANNING ITS CIRCULATION. THE PIECE MAY NEVER BE PLAYED AGAIN!

AND THE CENTRAL COMMITTEE IS DEMANDING YOU PUBLICLY DISAVOW THE WORK!

DISAVOW "CREDO"?

UNDER NO CIRCUMSTANCES!

WHEN I COMPOSED "CREDO," I BELIEVED JESUS' WORDS "YE RESIST NOT EVIL" ...

... COULD BE CONVEYED INTO MUSICAL FORM.

BUT EVIL IS STILL WRITTEN INTO MY MUSIC!

IT'S LIKE FINDING YOURSELF ON A DEAD-END STREET — YOU MUST BREAK THROUGH A WALL TO CONTINUE.

# PLOUGH BOOKLIST

**Subscribers 30% discount:** use code **PQ30** at checkout.

**Members 50% discount:** call for code or check your members-only newsletter. Plough Members automatically get new Plough books. Learn more at *plough.com/members*.

## Graphic Novels

### Between Two Sounds
Arvo Pärt's Journey to His Musical Language
*Joonas Sildre, translated by Adam Cullen*

A graphic novel follows the celebrated Estonian composer through the cultural, political, personal, and spiritual upheavals that led to the distinctive style that made him the most performed living composer in the world.

"Sildre's exceptional biography of the experimental Estonian composer finds novel ways to visualize his revolutionary sound. The comic's storytelling translates the minimalist beauty and power of Pärt's music to the page. . . . Lovers of art and music will be inspired."
**—*Publisher's Weekly,* starred review**

Hardcover, 224 pages, ~~$26.00~~ **$18.20 with subscriber discount**

### Freiheit!
The White Rose Graphic Novel
*Andrea Grosso Ciponte*

Delve deeper into the dramatic true story of a handful of students who resisted the Nazis and paid with their lives.

"A heartfelt, well-deserved tribute."
**—*Kirkus Reviews***

Hardcover, 112 pages, ~~$24.00~~ **$16.80 with subscriber discount**

### Mandela and the General
*John Carlin and Oriol Malet*

The struggle for racial justice will be won when we win over our adversaries. Find out how Nelson Mandela earned the trust of a white nationalist leader.

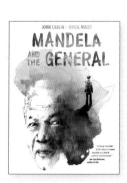

"A riveting read. Carlin captures powerfully Mandela's political astuteness and vast generosity."
**—Morgan Freeman**

Hardcover, 112 pages, ~~$19.95~~ **$13.97 with subscriber discount**

# The Busted Bean

*Follow an old school bus's transformation into a space
for coffee and camaraderie.*

**MAUREEN SWINGER**

THE OLD WHITE BUS looked so lonely sitting out by the farm, far from the school kids it used to haul around the Hudson Valley on day trips and camping excursions. But our community mechanic was clear – its driving days were over. It had been rusting in the lot for two years waiting for someone to buy it at a pathetic price for parts, or at least its Mercedes engine. When no bidders came along, my husband, Jason, walked around it a few times and made an offer.

Our dream was to renovate it into a coffee bus, providing it could limp up the hill to Coleman Corners on the southwest edge of Fox Hill Bruderhof. (Coleman Corners is the farm stand we started in the early days of the pandemic so that we could still have some form of community with friends in the neighborhood. These friends currently number 831 – at least the ones who have signed up in the guest book for event notifications.)

Well, we got a thumbs-up for the project, and in May 2022 that sweet old vehicle drove – fitfully – up to the maintenance shed so the makeover could commence. First on the agenda: goodbye to those beat-up seats.

Then the luggage racks had to go, in preparation for roof-raising. This bus was definitely built for middle-schoolers – the average man barely had standing clearance. So Jason and a couple fired-up metalworkers, Max and Dylan, set about removing all the windows, cutting the frames to lift the roof sixteen inches, and adding extenders to support the higher ceiling.

Next the entire youth group arrived for a rust-removal party, one of many such times they lent their energy and inspiration to further the cause of coffee.

By July, the Busted Bean was ready for its victory lap, one loop around the ring road surrounding Fox Hill community, with all its makeover crew on board – or rather, above board.

Chugging up the hill to its final parking place, abutting the farm-stand shed, the bus settled in for the long haul.

We were hoping to get it weatherproof before winter so the interior could keep evolving during the cold, sleety days of November.

Our youngest daughter was a keen participant in the bus beautification process, and got an education in a bit of everything, from sealing plywood subfloors to painting the exterior in cappuccino colors and sanding and staining the wheelchair ramp.

Jason, Max, and Dylan planed and shaped the wood for the interior paneling for the walls and ceiling.

As winter settled in, so did the floors, in late-night and early-morning projects by the glow of the newly wired recessed lighting, powered from a nearby telephone pole. (Thank you, Perrin and Leroy.)

Leonard and sons came over from Woodcrest community to design and build the cabinetry, and help Jason build miniature cantilevered tables jutting out from the bus walls.

The coffee counter forms a wall behind the original driver's seat and dashboard, but kids can still get to it via the old bus stairs up front. Many imaginary miles can be traversed thereby, with the passengers in back completely unaware of the journey.

Carl, a friend who is good at scrounging up amazing finds, discovered the never-assembled pieces of eight golden-age speakeasy bar stools

---

*Maureen Swinger is a senior editor at* Plough *and lives at the Fox Hill Bruderhof in Walden, New York, with her husband, Jason, and their three children.*

in an old movie prop warehouse, and talked the owner into donating them. Jason assembled and stained them, then asked a textile engineer to coach him through the upholstery process. (Thank you, Ben.) Later online browsing led us to discover similar chairs being sold for $1,000 each, helping us appreciate the contributions of scroungers, carpenters, and upholstery-coach friends all the more.

Jason had been having shoulder trouble for some time, and, just as the end of renovation was in sight, he was scheduled for surgery to fix a torn rotator cuff. Suddenly he was working every spare minute up to the hospital date to get the big stuff done before being grounded. Post-surgery, he took note of the stern warning not to move his arm away from his side and turned his attention to interior decor, discovering that it is possible to wood-burn classic coffee quotes into cherry panels while absolutely not moving one's shoulder.

We put our heads together with other interested parties to narrow down our equipment choices. Considering that farm-stand events can draw hundreds of visitors, we opted for a simple, sturdy, industrial coffeemaker rather than a fancy espresso machine, though that may yet be in the offing someday. We decided to use high quality, ethically sourced coffee beans, ground immediately before brewing, and add frothed milk for lattes and cappuccinos to get the best taste for the most people.

Almost to the exact hour of the Busted Bean's second birthday, the doors opened for the first neighborhood coffee event, attended by 180 farm-stand friends, sipping and chatting, picking their favorite coffee quotes on the walls and *Plough* books on the shelves.

Since then, it's been host to a neighborhood interfaith gathering as well as a small Bible study group. It has witnessed wild '60s-themed birthday parties (looking at you, Sue) and offered Sunday post-service coffees for anyone walking by. I love to stand at the counter as someone steps in for the first time. I imagine the bus must get some satisfaction out of it as well; after all, buses are meant to have all seats filled. ➢

# Jakob Hutter
## A Man Free in Christ

**EMMY BARTH MAENDEL and SUSANNAH BLACK ROBERTS**

*The sixteenth-century martyr fought tirelessly for truth.*

IT WAS THE FEAST OF the Ascension in May of 1535, when Jakob Hutter, his wife, and his companions were driven out of Auspitz, a small vineyard town in the south of Moravia in today's Czechia.

The congregation had been safe in Moravia for more than half a decade at that point, free to practice their Anabaptist faith according to the dictates of their consciences. This was due to the groundwork that Jan Hus had laid one hundred years before. Many of the Moravian nobles were Hussites, and had been so for one hundred years, the remnants of that Reformation *avant la lettre*, and they extended protection to their younger brothers.

But Moravia was still, for all its tradition of tolerance, part of the Kingdom of Bohemia, itself a vassal state of the Holy Roman Empire. The King of Bohemia was the Habsburg Archduke Ferdinand I. And Ferdinand was nervous.

*Emmy Barth Maendel is a member of the Bruderhof and a senior archivist for the Bruderhof's historical archives. Susannah Black Roberts is a senior editor at* Plough.

Photograph by Agata Kadar.

Justine Maendel, *Jakob Hutter*, oil on board, 2023

In 1525, the peasants of Central Europe had rebelled with shocking violence all the more disturbing because it was decentralized. That rebellion had had something to do with the new doctrines, though Martin Luther had condemned it roundly. In 1533, not far away in Münster, the fanatical and not-at-all-pacifist Anabaptist Jan van Leiden had taken over the city and begun running it as an oppressive theocracy; only with great difficulty was the city retaken.

Ferdinand was taking no chances in his realm of Bohemia. He himself attended the diet of 1535, demanding that the Moravian nobility stop running interference for their little brothers, the Anabaptists, and expel them.

This heavy-handed rule was something that the Moravians had objected to even before their Hussite awakening: Moravian freedoms, it was felt, had been under attack for centuries. But in the face of Ferdinand's demand, there was nothing to be done. Hutter, the leader of the congregation that had taken refuge in Auspitz for the past two years, packed what he could carry on his back, as did the rest of his flock, and left town. As the Hutterite histories recount, they were driven into the open fields like a herd of sheep, not permitted to camp anywhere until they reached the village of Tracht, where they slept on the wide heath under the open sky. Many widows, children, and sick people were in their number. Hutter wrote to the governor Kuna von Kunstadt:

> Now we find ourselves out in the wilderness, in a desolate meadow with no one being harmed. We do not want to cause anyone suffering or wrong, not even our worst enemy. What we preach is what we speak: to live in peace and unity in God's truth and justice. We are not ashamed of giving an account of ourselves to anyone. But whoever says that we took possession of the field with so many thousands, as if we were going to war, is a lying scoundrel. If all the world were like us there would be no war and no injustice. May God in heaven

show us where to go. We cannot be denied a place on earth, for the earth is the Lord's.

JAKOB HUTTER WAS BORN around 1500 in the village of Moos, in what is now South Tyrol, Italy; at the time, it was in Austria. He had no formal education, but learned the trade of a hatter. In the late 1520s he discovered the New Testament through the teachings of an itinerant preacher, a former goatherd called Wölfl. Little is known of Hutter's own journey, but by 1529 he was considered by the authorities, at least locally, to be a significant leader of the new Anabaptist sect. His countrymen, moved by his new presentation of the gospel, listened to him, and he baptized many of them, forming several congregations in the region.

The Anabaptist revival that spread like a wildfire across southern Germany and Austria did not go unnoticed. In 1527, King Ferdinand I proclaimed that the doctrines and practices of the Anabaptists would not be tolerated. People who had themselves baptized were imprisoned; those who baptized them were executed.

In response to this tyranny, Hutter went with a friend to investigate rumors that in Moravia Anabaptists could practice their faith free from fear. He returned with good news. As the *Chronicle of the Hutterian Brethren* puts it, the Anabaptists of Austerlitz "were of one heart and soul in serving and fearing God. Thereupon Jakob [and his] companions, in the name of the whole church, united in peace with the church at Austerlitz."

At this news, many of the Tyrolian converts began to head east – families and small groups, in twos and threes, more leaving every day to make the six-hundred-odd kilometer journey to what they hoped would be a safe haven. Hutter, however, felt that his calling – at least for the moment – was to remain in Tyrol and continue to minister to his converts there.

He made several trips to Moravia over the next few years. Free from persecution, the Anabaptists there were now struggling to maintain unity under leaders who, Hutter found, were making a hash of it. There was excess severity in some cases, with innocents being subject to church discipline, and laxity in others, where leaders "allowed for fleshly

---

## "This fire will harm my soul as little as the fiery furnace harmed Shadrach, Meshach, and Abednego." —Jakob Hutter

---

freedom in various ways, each taking control of their own possessions, as it suited them." In summer 1533 Hutter moved to Auspitz, Moravia, and brought order to the community there: he was beloved and considered a fair mediator.

The next two years were a time of spiritual maturing for the Anabaptists. Hutter was a gifted leader, and many of the squabbles which had plagued the church before he came melted away. The joy of the community, now well-shepherded, is palpable in Hutter's letters. He was happy, of course, that they were free of persecution, but happier still that they were no longer in spiritual perplexity, that the community had not succumbed to the slavery of personal ambition or disorder. As he wrote to those in Tyrol:

> For the first time, the Lord is truly freeing the devout hearts and consciences from human worries, delivering them from bondage. . . . Christ has liberated them all and set them free. . . . Have no doubt that the only freedom we can have is the freedom of Christ, not the freedom of the flesh. We are made free by God alone through Christ, redeemed and saved in our hearts by the Holy Spirit.

Those two years were a respite for Hutter and his community, and the group that emerged from that time would later be called Hutterites after the man who had led them.

But then, trouble. Because of the disaster of the "Anabaptist" takeover of Münster, King Ferdinand clamped down on Anabaptists everywhere,

and even the landowners in Moravia were commanded to expel them. Hutter had written a scathing letter to the Moravian governor and now his life was in danger. He returned to Tyrol with his wife, Katharina.

Immediately he began evangelizing again, and more were added to their number even in this least auspicious of moments. "The ungodly tyrants," he wrote in a letter home to Moravia, "do not yet know that we are here. God grant that they do not find it out."

But they did find out. A warrant was issued for Hutter's arrest. On November 30, 1535, he and Katharina were arrested in a friend's house in Klausen and taken to Branzoll Castle.

Hutter was then transferred to Innsbruck, where he was cross-examined. A Catholic academic, Dr. Gallus Müller, attempted to reconcile him to Catholicism, using proofs from the scriptures. Hutter did not budge.

Over the next few months, he was tortured repeatedly. His captors put him in ice-cold water, then beat him with rods. They slashed his body, poured brandy into his cuts, and then set the brandy on fire. On February 25, 1536, they burnt him at the stake in Innsbruck. "Come closer, those of you who contradict me!" he called out. "Let us test our faith in the fire. This fire will harm my soul as little as the fiery furnace harmed Shadrach, Meshach, and Abednego."

"He gave a great sermon through his death," wrote Hans Amon, a contemporary Hutterite, "for God was with him."

Katharina had likewise refused to recant, but after several months she gave her captors the slip. She worked on for two more years before she was finally recaptured and executed, likely by drowning.

Hutter's execution, of course, marked him as a martyr. But there were many martyrs in those days. Hutter glorified God not only in his death, but in the life that he lived, as he led his brothers into the freedom that Christ had bought for them. ⤳

Photograph by Melinda Barth. Used by permission.